BEGINNING
SWIMMING

M. M. MACKENZIE
Teachers College
Columbia University

BETTY SPEARS
Wellesley College

WADSWORTH PUBLISHING COMPANY, INC.
Belmont, California

Sixth Printing, April 1966

L. C. Cat. Card No.: 62-10394

Printed in the United States of America

CONTENTS

UNDERSTANDING
THE SPORT OF SWIMMING

1

WHY SWIM?

Safety

For your own safety, as well as for the safety of your family and others, you should learn to swim. Safety in and around water has become a necessity in daily life. The increase in the number of backyard pools and the growth of the boating industry and its allied sport activities place each person in a position where swimming is a must. It is embarrassing to refuse to participate, but foolhardy to engage in water sports, if you cannot swim. Swimming safely and well provides skills that last a lifetime.

History

Swimming is as old as humanity and has been a part of the culture of many civilizations and nations. Earliest records of swimming date back to the year 9000 B.C., when pictures of swimmers were etched on the walls of caves in the Libyan Desert. History reveals that swimming has been closely associated with the military training, ceremonial and religious activities, and recreational life of many nations. In America, Benjamin Franklin was one of the earliest proponents of learning to swim.

For centuries swimming has provided fun, fitness, and friendships for the peoples of the world. Today, aquatic sport offers a vast area of exciting activity to those who swim.

Fun

You need only to watch people at a beach or pool to know that swimming is fun. Children scream with glee and romp for joy, boys and girls tease and joke, and men and women frolic with youthful vigor. The mystery of the water creates an atmosphere of excitement. The change of pace from daily life offers enjoyment and relaxation— a real need in today's tense and routine life. Swimming also opens the door to many recreational aquatic activities such as water skiing, boating, synchronized swimming, and skin diving.

1

Fitness

Few sports contribute as much as swimming does to the development of physical fitness. Swimming is particularly suited to fitness for women because the muscles are stretched rather than bunched. This stretching tends to produce a pleasing, feminine body. Swimming can build muscular strength, organic power, and endurance. Swimming for fitness has a very real meaning for many persons who are physically handicapped and restricted from many other sports.

Friendships

No matter what your age, you always can enjoy swimming and other aquatic activities. But, YOU SHOULD NEVER SWIM ALONE. This important safety slogan changes an apparently individual activity to a group sport, through which friendships can be made and fostered. Swimming is one of the most popular family sports and provides a means for increasing family solidarity.

An Inexpensive Sport

Since swimming requires little personal equipment beyond a suit, a bathing cap for girls and women, and a nose clip if desired, expenses are negligible. Special equipment such as kickboards and safety devices are available at most pools. Although fins and other equipment are available to swimmers, they are not necessary for learning to swim with a high degree of proficiency.

These, then, are the reasons for swimming. It is a safety skill, it is inexpensive, and it provides you with opportunities for having fun, maintaining fitness, and making friends.

WHEN AND WHEN NOT TO SWIM

As enthusiastic as we are about swimming, we must point out that there are times to swim and times *not* to swim. For your own health and safety know your limitations, know good swimming hygiene, and know the conditions under which you are swimming.

Know Your Limitations

Personal safety and the safety of others are the obligations of all swimmers. Can you handle the surf? Shall you participate in canoeing and rowboating? Shall you go deep-sea fishing? How far can you swim without tiring? Can you assist someone else who is having trouble in the water? All of these questions are extremely important for safe participation in swimming activities. Each person must know his capabilities and limitations. In Chapter 7 there is a Beginning Swimmer Check List. Test yourself and see how safe you are as a swimmer.

Swimming Hygiene

Safeguarding health while swimming is vital. Do this by having periodic medical checkups and observing hygienic practices relating to such things as showers, foot care, infections, and the like.

Medical examination. Because swimming can be a very vigorous activity, it is important to have a clean bill of health from a physician. Having routine, annual physical examinations is a wise procedure in this regard. Request specifically the physician's permission to swim. Then his examination helps him to spot conditions that might prevent or limit participation. If your health history reveals heart disease, ear or sinus infection, or epilepsy, it is likely that a reduced amount of swimming activity will be recommended.

Infections. If you are suffering from any infections or open wounds, do not swim. Sometimes infections of the ear, particularly the middle ear and the sinus cavities, are attributed to swimming. These may be avoided by use of proper methods in the equalization of pressures in the nasal passages. Practice the breathing techniques recommended in Chapter 2 to avoid infection and restricted activity in the water.

Showers. Shower thoroughly with soap and water after using the toilet and before donning your suit and entering the pool. Such a practice is necessary to reduce the spread of infection as well as to permit the water filtration and purification system to work at its best.

Menstrual hygiene. Most pool regulations state that girls and women should not use the pool during their menstrual period. Cold water has been found to have an adverse reaction on some individuals. Medical opinion differs as to the use of internal protection. Specific problems should be guided by the advice of a physician.

Foot care. Sandals should be worn to prevent the feet from getting dirty while walking to and from the bathing area. Dry the feet thoroughly after swimming or bathing and wear only clean socks. The use of a foot powder might be helpful in keeping the feet dry. Such symptoms as skin peeling, itching, or cracking between the toes should be checked by a competent physician.

Swimming after meals. Today people still talk about the myth that swimming immediately after eating causes stomach cramps which in turn lead to drowning. There is no scientific evidence to prove or disprove this theory. Resting after each meal for approximately 60–90 minutes, regardless of the activity which might follow, is just common sense.

Cramps. A cramp is a very rapid expansion and contraction of a muscle or a group of muscles usually accompanied by severe pain, which results in a knotting of the muscles involved. Cramps usually occur in the foot or calf, and occasionally develop in the back of the thigh, the hand and the upper arm. Cramps are caused by at least three conditions: (1) fatigue, (2) cold water, and (3) sudden action of the muscles involved. There may be other causes still unknown to medical authorities. To RELEASE A CRAMP, STRETCH AND GENTLY MASSAGE OR KNEAD THE CRAMPED MUSCLES.

Sunburn. The appeal of acquiring a healthy-looking sun tan sometimes relaxes common sense and results in the painful experience of sunburn. Severe sunburn not only causes illness but also may restrict your activity for many days, depriving you of the fun of the out-of-doors. Sunburn may occur on hazy days and may be acquired indirectly from the reflection of the sun's rays upon water or a light-colored surface such as sand. Merely sitting under an umbrella at the beach will not prevent sunburn. Although there are many lotions advertised to prevent sunburn, and there are a few that do, the best preventative is to regulate the amount of time spent exposed to the sun's rays. This may vary from twenty minutes to several hours, depending upon your susceptibility at a given time.

Bathing caps. Women wear bathing caps in pools to prevent a collection of hair from clogging the filters. A bathing cap also serves to keep the hair out of the eyes and permits swimming without annoyance or handicap.

SCIENTIFIC FACTS ABOUT SWIMMING

Learning to swim will proceed much more rapidly if the swimmer understands both the psychological problems that beginning swimmers face and the principles of movement and physiological capabilities and limitations of the body in water.

Psychological Facts

Recognize that learning to swim takes time—a lot of it. Many persons lose their enthusiasm because they expect miracles immediately. By setting out on a slow but steady pace, satisfaction will be yours. Don't expect to perform like an Olympic swimmer overnight; be satisfied with developing the fundamentals and gradually improving your skill with practice. To develop excellence in swimming, for young and old alike, takes years of practice.

The best swimming instructor in the world will be of little value if you do not enter into learning to swim with a clear picture of what is ahead. Prepare yourself mentally to proceed from a non-swimmer to a swimmer who is safe in deep water. Do not be afraid to face fear and embarrassment as a beginner, and recognize the problems of communication and space orientation. These problems are *common* to beginning swimmers. Patience and a desire to learn will help a great deal in overcoming them.

Fear. Face up to the fact that water presents elements of danger to the beginner, *as well as to the accomplished swimmer.* Recognize that you are not alone in having a real sense of fear. Fear is a basic emotion that stems from a desire for survival. Man fears most the things or situations that he does not understand.

Fear can be helpful in motivating you to learn new skills. It also stimulates physiological processes by releasing chemicals that allow you to exert more strength. On the other hand, fear can work negatively by causing you to panic, to "lose your head," and to dissipate large amounts of energy. Exhaustion then sets in and the skills you have learned cannot be used to protect you.

Don't try to hide your fear of the water. The instructor knows beginning swimmers may be afraid and he will do everything possible to eliminate dangerous situations. The aquatic experiences he organizes are designed to help you face fear in a positive and realistic way. Have confidence in his ability and *know* that fear can be overcome.

Embarrassment. Embarrassment is felt by all people at some time during their life. Having to admit to inability to swim or having to refuse to join in water sports causes many persons a great deal of embarrassment, which can be compounded when a young man or woman must reveal this inadequacy to members of the opposite sex. This is particularly true among men, who, in our society, are supposed to be dominant. One might also be embarrassed because beginning swimming movements feel awkward. Any new movements seem awkward until they become familiar. These feelings will be overcome as the beginner learns to swim adequately.

Communication. Communication in swimming is different from communication in other sports. In swimming the problems of getting ideas from the instructor to the learner are sometimes complicated because of terminology unique to swimming and a feeling of isolation. When an instructor uses the terms *up* and *down*, he means these directions in relation to the body while standing (the position most familiar to you). *Up* means toward the ceiling. The terms *front* and *over the head* mean a horizontal position or movement in the direction in which you are moving in the water. The terms *in* and *out* are used in relation to the midline of the body running from head to toe. Thus, if instructed to move your hands *in*, move them toward the center line of your body. To aid in understanding swimming terminology, Chapter 8 is a glossary of swimming terms.

Isolation caused by submerging the eyes and ears under water also causes communication problems. With your face under water you are on your own when you most need to see the reassuring presence and to hear the instructive words of your teacher. Words of encouragement and correction cannot be heard. However, this situation forces you to remember instructions and suggestions and to become self-sufficient as quickly as possible. As a beginning swimmer, recognize the positive and negative aspects of this concept of communicative isolation in order to make your learning more rapid.

Noise is another factor which sometimes interferes with communication in swimming instruction. Voices are raised because of the sound of splashing water and because many swimmers are likely to be wearing bathing caps or to have water in their ears. Be as quiet and attentive as possible to assist the instructor in making swimming fun and safe for everyone.

Space orientation. While most of the activities in daily life are performed in an upright position, swimming is done horizontally with the effect of gravity reduced because of the water. This requires that you re-orient your body in space, which sometimes results in a degree of confusion. First, it is difficult to correct wrong movements because the sense of balance is distorted. The brain is accustomed to interpreting balance stimuli in relation to the normal pull of gravity with the body in an upright position.

Second, confusion occurs because the legs trail behind, out of sight. In most activities you can see what your legs are doing and are able to make corrections readily. But if you try to look at your legs while swimming you destroy the proper total body position and create major problems in stroke execution. This means that you must learn by feeling (kinesthetic sense). Since this is a new experience it slows the learning process. Yet its newness provides a challenge.

Physiological Facts

Although for convenience and clarity we treat the areas of psychology and physiology separately, they are closely related. Man, composed of interdependent mental and physical processes, performs, lives, and experiences as a total being. Movement without thought is impossible, just as thought, without the physical processes of the nervous system and the reception of stimuli, is impossible. Important physiological concepts to be understood include relaxation, fatigue, breathing, and body build.

Relaxation. The relaxation of muscles is closely associated with the mental state. Fear and anxiety contribute to tense muscles, causing the arms, legs, and back to be rigid. Tense, rigid muscles cause two major difficulties in swimming: improper movement and fatigue. Rigid muscles prevent the body joints—the elbows, shoulders, knees, ankles, and neck—from moving. Movement or exertion of force cannot take place without some joint action. Try this experiment: Hold one arm extended in front of the body at shoulder height. Tense the muscles and hold the arm rigid. Now, try to bend the elbow. It is impossible! This simple experiment should prove that tense muscles prevent movement.

Relaxation is one of the keys to swimming, as it is to all other physical activity. The highly skilled athlete performs in an easy, apparently effortless manner to which we apply the term *relaxed.* Relaxation in swimming means using only those muscles needed to exert force—no more, no less—and keeping those muscles loose or "relaxed." Be confident and patient, and proceed with learning to swim in an easy manner, both mentally and physically.

Fatigue. If you work too hard at executing a skill or hold the muscles tense, you will tire in a very short time. Water resistance increases in proportion to the amount of force executed against it. Try moving an arm slowly through the water and note how easy it is to do this. Now move the arm as quickly as possible through the water. There is quite a difference in resistance. To overcome this resistance requires energy, which in due time is used up; fatigue then sets in.

The more fatigued you are, the more difficult it becomes to execute movements correctly. Correct movements in the water require that force be exerted against maximum resistance. If you are tired, it will be natural to follow the path of least resistance. This will hinder correct learning. For further information on the principles of physics which control movement, see the section immediately following.

Fatigue also numbs the desire to learn. It is important to spread the expenditure of energy over each period of instruction. Expect to be tired during the first few lessons. Gradually, as you swim more and more, your endurance in the water will improve.

Breathing. Comfortable and useful aquatic breathing is one of the most difficult of all swimming skills. Breathing in a new way, coordinating the breathing cycle with the movements of arms and legs, and overcoming a concern about not getting air, make aquatic breathing a natural stumbling block. It is essential that everyone master this technique. Normal breathing is done through the nose with little or no effort. Aquatic breathing consists of breathing only through the mouth and exhaling through the mouth or nose and mouth. Breathing while swimming must be rhythmical in order to provide the body with a constant supply of oxygen. Aquatic breathing comes only with repeated practice. The details of breath control are explained in Chapter 2.

Facts from the Science of Physics

An understanding of some of the basic principles of physics is necessary in learning to swim safely and quickly. Certain concepts of body coordination are presented below. Other laws of physics that are applicable to swimming are related to such things as levers, hydrodynamics, cavitation, acceleration, streamlining, planing, hydrofoils, and the like. Unfortunately there is insufficient research evidence upon which to base any scientific conclusions. The basic principles presented below should develop a more complete understanding of swimming.

Motion. Newton's Third Law of Motion is applicable particularly to swimming. This law states that for every action there is an equal and opposite reaction. When a pistol is fired, there is a kick-back or recoil. Similarly when pressure is exerted against the water, the water resists this pressure in proportion to the amount of force exerted. The harder the force against the water, the more resistance the water gives, resulting in more speed. The direction of movement will be in a direction opposite to the pressure. In swimming then, it is important to apply force exactly opposite to the direction in which you wish to move. This knowledge will help you avoid any action that does not move you where you want to go.

Force and power. You have just learned that to move in one direction it is necessary to apply force in the opposite direction. This is not always possible. Many movements in swimming capitalize on resultant forces rather than on opposite forces. For example, one of the most common kicks used in swimming is the crawl kick, in which the legs alternately thrash up and down. An up motion theoretically sends the body down, and a down motion pushes the body up. But you want to go forward, not up or down. Now, these up-and-down thrashes exert a number of forces at various angles. Although some of the effort is lost, there is a resultant force, less than the total, which propels the body in the desired direction—forward.

Swimming strokes are analyzed in cycles. Each cycle consists of one complete arm and leg movement. Within each cycle is a "recovery" phase and a "power" phase. The recovery phase comprises the movements necessary for the arms or legs to be ready to apply power. The power phase is the application of force to the water by the arms or legs. Exert as much force as possible during the power phase; eliminate or minimize force during the recovery phase.

Often the beginning swimmer believes that he moves faster in the water if his movements are rapid. This is true if, at the same time, force is applied in the proper direction. However, as the pace of the stroke cycle is increased, the muscles tend to become tense and rigid and the arm action "slips" out of the path of maximum resistance, losing power and thus speed. To swim faster, concentrate on increasing power, rather than on increasing the stroke tempo.

Buoyancy. The force which appears to hold the body up in water is known as buoyancy. Archimedes' principle states that when a body is placed in a fluid, the weight it appears to lose is equal to the weight of the fluid it displaces. We are interested in this principle for three reasons. First, practically all human beings have a specific gravity less than that of water, and, therefore, will float. It is necessary to place the body in the correct positions for floating and to keep the lungs inflated, BUT THE WATER DOES HOLD THE BODY UP. (See Chapter

2 for an explanation of floating.) This concept is important when executing the back float, for without much effort the nose and mouth can be kept above water in a safe position.

Second, if the head or other parts of the body are *completely* out of water, gravity is working against buoyancy. Your head weighs between 12 and 15 pounds. It stands to reason that as much of the head and body as possible should be kept in the water to make use of the effect of buoyancy. By maintaining the body in the correct position under the water, the propelling forces of the arms and legs do not have as much gravitational pull to overcome.

Third, human beings differ in body build and thus have varying centers of gravity and different floating positions. For example, a "pleasingly plump" girl of average height generally floats in a horizontal position, while a lean, six-foot man usually floats with his feet well underwater. These facts indicate that the body position for executing swimming skills and strokes varies from person to person, depending upon body build. Do not be surprised when your instructor suggests individual adaptations for the various skills. Your teacher knows how to adjust each technique so that you may swim as safely and quickly as possible.

Coordination. Along with relaxation, coordination is one of the keys to excellence in physical performance. Execute strokes or skills with proper timing so that the muscles work in harmony and the body remains balanced around its center of gravity. The terms *rhythm* and *balance* might be used in place of the term *coordination*. Certain patterns of swimming movement are called strokes and promote efficiency. These strokes are presented in Chapter 3.

FROM NON-SWIMMER TO SWIMMER

You are now ready to learn how to swim. Learning to swim is accomplished by building upon your abilities step by step in a natural learning progression. Listed below are nine steps to becoming a safe swimmer. Each of these steps is discussed in detail in this chapter.

Step 1—Breath Control
Step 2—Prone Floats
Step 3—Human Stroke
Step 4—Back Float
Step 5—Beginning Backstroke
Step 6—Position Changes
Step 7—Treading Water
Step 8—Water Entries
Step 9—Evaluation

If you are enrolled in a swimming course, do not be surprised to find that your instructor uses a class progression other than the one presented here. Depending upon the initial fear of the beginning swimmer, the size of the group, and other particulars, each teacher will present the material somewhat differently. For example, learning the back float and the beginning backstroke might precede learning the face floats and the human stroke. Students who are afraid will naturally progress somewhat more slowly.

PRACTICE GUIDES

In addition to class instruction, you will need to practice by yourself to become proficient, ASSUMING OF COURSE THAT A LIFE GUARD IS PRESENT. To facilitate practice it is important to plan time carefully, to set realistic objectives, to use written materials wisely, to engage in appropriate drills and to understand when to enter deep water.

Time Schedule

At least 45 minutes of daily practice is advocated. The amount of time spent at practicing various skills and strokes will vary from one person to another depending upon their performance strengths or weaknesses. The following time schedule is suggested:

10 minutes—Review of written materials pertaining to activities to be practiced.

5 minutes—Warmup activities—dry-land stretching exercises; rhythmical breathing and bobbing; floating, kicking, and arm-stroking drills.

10 minutes—Practice of skills already learned to improve or maintain proficiency.

15 minutes—Practice of new skills introduced in class during the current week.

5 minutes—Swim for distance and time using as many different strokes as possible.

Learning Progressions

To assist you further in planning your practice schedule an eight-week series of learning progressions is presented below. These progressions are based upon the assumption that there will be instruction three days per week and out-of-class practice on the alternate days.

In Chapter 7 you will find a list of weekly performance objectives which an average adult can reasonably expect to reach. Concentrate on attaining *all* of the objectives listed for each week. This means that only a few minutes or seconds might be spent at practicing some skills, while considerable time will be devoted to perfecting other skills.

First Week

Review: None
New: Step 1—breath holding, rhythmical breathing, bobbing; Step 2—tuck float and recovery, face float and glide and recovery; Step 3—human stroke; Step 4—back float and recovery.

Second Week

Review: Steps 1 through 4
New: Step 5—sculling, backstroke kick; Step 6—turning around while swimming the human stroke and beginning backstroke; turning from the beginning backstroke to the human stroke and vice versa; Step 7—treading water (in neck-deep water).

Third Week

Review: Steps 1 through 7
New: Step 8—jumping into chest-deep water, jump and swim in deep water *with supervision*, diving from edge of pool.

Fourth Week
> Review: Steps 1 through 8
> New: Step 9—Composite Skill Test, jump from 1-meter board.

Fifth Week
> Review: Steps 1 through 9
> New: Elementary backstroke, crawl.

Sixth Week
> Review: Step 9, diving, elementary backstroke, and crawl.
> New: Sidestroke, drownproofing.

Seventh Week
> Review: Drownproofing, all strokes, jumping, diving, and treading water.
> New: Breaststroke, underwater swimming, surface dive.

Eighth Week
> Review: All skills previously learned.
> New: Progressive bobbing, crawl, and butterfly.

Use of Text

Periodic review of the information presented throughout this book should prove helpful as you undergo practice periods. The scientific facts about swimming (see page 4ff.) will become more meaningful as you increase your swimming ability. Therefore a rereading of this information every week or two will help you to correct mistakes due to a violation of or lack of understanding about the fundamental principles related to swimming. Pre-practice reading of stroke and skill descriptions is also recommended. This will serve to focus your attention on essential movements.

Drills

The drills to be followed during practice should be patterned after those presented by your instructor during class. These drills vary from skill to skill and from one instructor to another. There is no best method for learning a particular skill. What works for one learner may not for another. Thus during practice you should experiment with all of the techniques used in class and find those most suitable to you. In the beginning stages plan practice drills to move toward shore or the side of the pool. Be careful not to move into deep water or in water where you will be unsafe.

Several suggested learning techniques for various skills are presented in this text. Others may be found in the references cited on page 87. When practicing strokes, separate practice is needed for learning the leg action, arm action, coordinated arm and leg action without breathing, coordinated arm and breathing action, and total stroke coordination.

Practicing the leg action (the backstroke excepted) may be accomplished by using the kickboard or by holding on to the side of the pool. The arm action may be practiced before a mirror to check proper movement. Arm action may also be practiced when standing in shallow water (the backstroke excepted), with the body bent at the hips so that the torso and head are in the water. In addition, arm action may be practiced by letting the legs trail, buoyed up with a partially inflated rubber ball held between the legs, while swimming.

Often it is advisable to practice a stroke without breathing, that is, by holding the breath. The swimmer, then, can concentrate on proper arm-leg coordination without interference from interrupted breathing. As proficiency is developed, breathing is introduced into the coordinated stroke.

The breathing cycle of a stroke is learned best by relating it to the arm stroke. This may be accomplished through dry-land drills or shallow-water practice. In both cases the learner stands but keeps the torso in the horizontal swimming position. The arms are moved slowly without force as the breathing cycle is coordinated appropriately. Once the breathing is related to the arms in the drill situations, the learner attempts the total coordination while swimming.

Deep-Water Swimming

The sooner you try out deep water the better, but ONLY WITH THE APPROVAL AND SUPERVISION OF AN INSTRUCTOR. Most adult beginners are ready for deep-water swimming during their second or third week of instruction. Some persons, particularly children, are capable of swimming in deep water during the second or third lesson. Your instructor will determine when you are ready for deep-water swimming, generally after you complete Step 7, "Treading Water" (see page 31.)

STEP 1: BREATH CONTROL

It is vital to your safety and comfort to control your breath when in and around water. When swimming INHALE ONLY THROUGH THE MOUTH AND EXHALE ONLY THROUGH THE MOUTH OR NOSE AND MOUTH.

Aquatic Breathing

Inhalation. When inhaling, make the effort quick yet strong, with the lips and teeth slightly parted. Control this effort primarily with the chest muscles, without gasping. When you gasp for air with the mouth wide open, water may enter the windpipe and discomfort will result. Initially, the "shipping" of water into the mouth while inhaling may be bothersome until you learn to let water collect under the tongue or in the side of the mouth. In time the presence of water will become no more troublesome than the presence of saliva or food in the mouth.

Exhalation. Exhaling air while swimming requires considerable control to overcome water pressure. Force air out through the mouth or nose and mouth in the form of bubbles in the water. Have a friend or partner watch for these bubbles. They actually can be seen. If water has collected in the mouth expel it with the air. During exhalation keep the lips *slightly* parted as the air is spewed out under water.

Two methods are used to prevent water from entering the nasal passages. The most effective method, although not always preferred, is the use of a nose clip. This simple rubber device squeezes the nostrils together, preventing air or water from entering the nose. The second method is to maintain a minimum amount of positive exhalation pressure at the base of the nasal passages. This is an acquired habit and for some persons difficult to learn. One uncomfortable and sometimes serious effect of water entering the nasal passages is inflammation of the sinus cavities. If you are unsuccessful in acquiring the habit of positive exhalation pressure very quickly, invest in a nose clip and be comfortable. Learning to swim does not proceed as rapidly as it should if there is discomfort.

Breath Holding

The ability to hold the breath is important in swimming since it develops confidence and permits the practice of many swimming skills. The technique of breath holding is primarily one of "mind over matter."

Practice Techniques

To master the skills mentioned above practice breath holding, rhythmical breathing, and bobbing.

Breath holding. Practice in chest-deep water, holding on to the overflow trough if necessary. With the head above water, inhale through the mouth only. Hold breath and submerge the face. Be careful not to breathe in through the nose. Keep the eyes open and relax the facial muscles. When the breath cannot be held any longer, slowly exhale through the mouth or through the nose and mouth. When all the air is expended, raise the face out of the water and inhale. Practice daily until you can hold your breath 60 seconds.

Rhythmical breathing. One technique for practicing breathing is to place the body in the prone (face down) position. In water not more than 2 feet deep, place the hands on the bottom directly under the shoulders with fingers spread and pointed straight ahead. Turn the head to one side and place the lower ear in the water, then inhale. Turn the head, allowing the face to submerge with the nose pointed straight down. Keep the eyes open. Exhale. Then turn the head to the side, keeping one ear in the water. Be sure the mouth is above the surface of the water. Inhale. Repeat the process again and again. This drill may be used later on in conjunction with practicing the crawl kick.

If shallow water is not available, breathing may be practiced in the prone position by holding on to the overflow trough. To position the body at the trough correctly, grasp the rim of the trough with one hand with the forearm (from wrist to elbow) placed underwater against the wall of the pool basin, elbow pointing down. Place the other hand, with fingers pointing downward, against the wall *directly below* the upper hand and approximately two feet below the surface of the water. Now push with the lower hand and pull with the upper hand until the body is extended on the surface of the water. Proceed with the breathing drill as described above for practice in very shallow water. Note also the illustrations below.

a   b

Fig. 1. Rhythmical Breathing: (a) hands on bottom in shallow water (b) holding on to overflow trough

Bobbing. Another means for developing skill in aquatic breathing is the technique of bobbing rhythmically up and down in the water. Start by standing in chest-deep water with feet spread and with one foot in front of the other. If support is needed (and this is sometimes true) practice by holding on to the overflow trough or to a partner's hand. As soon as you gain sufficient confidence, practice without support.

Assume the starting position described above and spread the arms at the surface of the water. Inhale. Then, keeping the back straight, bend the knees and allow the head to submerge. While under water, forcibly exhale through the mouth or nose and mouth. Keep the eyes open. After exhaling straighten the knees, gently press the arms down and return to a semi-standing position with the chin just above the surface of the water. Keep the back straight. Inhale. Immediately submerge. Repeat the process again and again, taking about 5 seconds for a complete cycle.

Fig. 2. Aquatic Breathing Practice

Proper aquatic breathing is one of the biggest problems for beginning swimmers. Many beginners make the mistake of inhaling rhythmically and not exhaling at all. They simply add more air each time they inhale until they can hold no more air. If you feel a tightness about your chest after six or seven breaths you probably are not exhaling. Another common error is to inhale too quickly as the face comes above the surface of the water. Many excellent swimmers finish exhaling just as their faces come out of water.

STEP 2: PRONE FLOATS

Learning to let the water support the body is the next step in learning to swim and, for many persons, the most important step of all. Body buoyancy is practiced in three positions: tuck, face or prone, and back.

Tuck Float

This float sometimes is called the "jelly fish" float and also is used as a buoyancy test. A buoyancy test is employed to demonstrate that water will support the weight of the body—that under normal conditions the body cannot sink. The unusual person who tends to float just *beneath* the surface of the water needs special help.

Start by standing in chest-deep water. Inhale deeply and hold the breath. Bend from the hips, place the chest and face in the water, and reach down with the hands to touch the shins. KEEP THE EYES OPEN. Now *slowly* bring the knees toward the chest and grasp the shins with the hands. If the lungs are full of air the water buoys the body up, lifting the feet from the bottom. Hold this position for as long as the breath can be held or as long as desired. Stay as relaxed as possible.

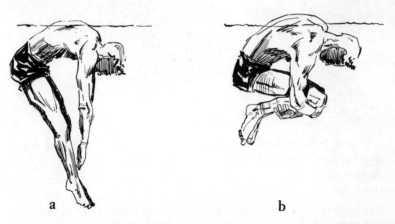

a   b

Fig. 3. Tuck Float Progression

There are two actions to remember in standing or recovering from
the tuck float: first, put the feet down on the bottom of the pool;
second, lift the head and bring the face above the surface of the
water.

The tuck float is the desired position to release a cramp in the
legs or arms. In this position stretch and gently massage the cramped
muscles with one or both hands.

Face Float and Glide

The face float and glide are the easiest skills to learn and are basic
to executing the crawl and breaststroke. Start in waist-deep water with
the back to the wall, with one foot on the bottom and one foot
placed underwater against the side of the pool, toes pointing downward and knee bent. Place the arms overhead, COVERING THE EARS
WITH THE UPPER PART OF YOUR ARMS, and interlock the thumbs. Inhale deeply, bend from the hips, and place the chest, face, and arms
in the water. Keep the eyes open. Gently, but firmly, push away from
the wall, allowing the body to glide forward on the surface with the
legs extended behind. Keep the head, hips, and heels (3 H's) at the
surface of the water. If the body tends to roll, bend the arms slightly
with elbows pointing outward to present a more stable surface on
the water.

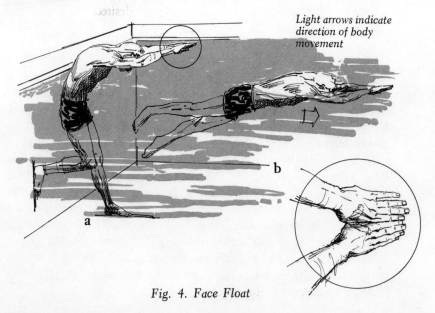

*Light arrows indicate
direction of body
movement*

Fig. 4. Face Float

To recover to the standing position in shallow water draw the knees to the chest, press the arms downward and the head back. Allow the body to sink until the feet touch the bottom. Then straighten the legs and stand up.

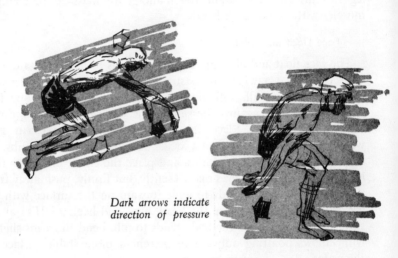

Dark arrows indicate
direction of pressure

Fig. 5. Recovery from Face Float

If you have difficulty in doing the face float and glide alone, a helper may give assistance by *gently supporting* the arms. The helper does this by standing three or four feet in front of and facing you. He gently grasps your wrists *from above*. As you glide forward he moves backward, maintaining minimum support of your wrists.

If the side of the pool is not used, execute the face float and glide from a standing position in waist- or chest-deep water. Spread the feet slightly and place one foot in front of the other. Bend the knees until the shoulders are under water. Extend the arms forward on the surface of the water, thumbs interlocked. Now inhale and drop the face into the water, covering the ears with the upper arms. Lean forward and firmly push upward and forward from the bottom into the prone, gliding position. Return to the standing position as described above.

STEP 3: HUMAN STROKE

Not all instructors agree that the human stroke, or dog paddle as it is often called, should be taught to the beginner. However, we are of the opinion that it should be one of the first strokes taught to adults since it does not require any sophisticated coordination of arms and legs and breathing.

Body Position

While swimming the human stroke, hold the body in the prone position with the head out of water and the chin just above the surface. Keep the hips and heels at the surface of the water and the shoulders rounded and hunched slightly forward. DON'T LET THE HIPS SAG. It takes strong lower back muscles to maintain the hips at the surface.

Arm Action

Move the arms alternately forward and backward in a vertical circle under water, as a dog moves its forepaws when swimming. This movement of the arms approximates that of the drive shaft on a locomotive.

Start with one arm partially extended about 15 inches in front of the head, fingers together, palm slightly cupped. Bend the elbow approximately 45 degrees (the arm is never completely straight at any time during the stroke). Keeping the forearm pointed directly ahead, press the water down and back with the palm and the underside of the forearm until the hand is under the chest. This completes the power action.

While one arm exerts power the other arm moves from the end of its power action to the beginning of another power action. Recover the arm under water by moving it to a position forward of the head, keeping palm down and elbow close to the body.

Leg Action

The leg action of the human stroke is an alternating, vertical whip-like motion, identical to that of the crawl stroke (see page 47 for illustrations of this kick).

Extend the legs behind, keeping toes pointed and turned in, thighs relaxed and KNEE AND ANKLE JOINTS LOOSE. Move the leg downward, describing an arc of about 15 degrees, with the knee leading and slightly bent. Straighten the knee at the end of the down-beat. Now lift the leg upward, kicking the foot *up* without raising it out of the water, in a whip-like action. As the feet pass, occasionally allow the big toes to rub against each other as a check to see that the feet are turned inward.

Breathing

Since the face is above water, breathing is no problem and is done at any time. Be sure to inhale through the mouth only.

Coordination

Allow the leg action to work easily into rhythm with the arm action. Memorize the arm-leg coordination: "right arm power, right leg down, left arm power, left leg down." There are two beats of the leg kick to each complete arm cycle. That is, the legs pass each other twice during the period that both of the arms execute their power action.

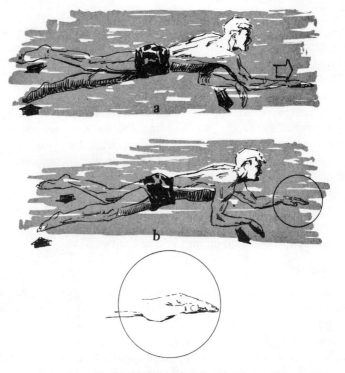

Fig. 6. Human Stroke Coordination

STEP 4: BACK FLOAT

The commonly used term *back float* is actually a misnomer, for most persons float in a semi-vertical position with their legs pointing toward the bottom of the pool. Depending upon the location of the center of gravity, the specific gravity of the body, and the amount of air that can be held in the lungs, the floating position ranges from the horizontal to the vertical. Women tend to float more in the horizontal position; most men float in a vertical position. To find your floating position, experiment with the placement of the arms and the arch of the back. Whatever your floating position may be, it is important that your nose and mouth remain *above* the surface of the water.

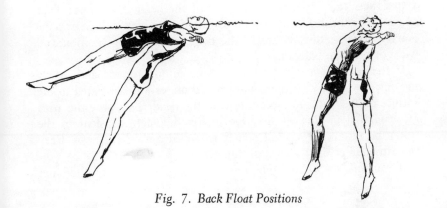

Fig. 7. Back Float Positions

Many beginners, hearing the term *back float*, start out in the horizontal position and become dismayed when they go right to the bottom. They do not realize that the density of their legs causes them to sink from the horizontal position. If most people will move gently into the proper position and wait for the body to find its balanced position, they will float. Experience indicates that less than one out of ten persons are really "sinkers." These people cannot float without a minimum amount of supplementary movement. (See page 25.)

Some assistance may be needed in learning the back float. THIS ASSISTANCE CONSISTS OF MINIMUM SUPPORT OF THE HEAD ONLY. A helper gently supports the head by placing one hand under the base of the skull while he is standing at the side of or behind the floater, out of the way of the outstretched arms, or by kneeling on the deck and reaching down to hold the head. The helper *gradually* removes the upward pressure, but always leaves his hand in position to assist if necessary.

To float on the back, start in a vertical position in neck-deep water. Place the stomach against the wall of the pool and hook the thumbs (only the thumbs) over the overflow trough. Arch the body (hips pressed forward) with toes pointed and the legs curled under and behind the body. Now with the lungs full of air put the head back, ears under water and the chin pointing to the ceiling, and slowly release your thumbs from the overflow trough so that the arms and hands are completely underwater. The only part of the body above the water is the face—about ⅛ of the head. Now if you float like a cork, the feet will come up. But if you have a high specific gravity, the legs already are in the neutral or floating position and will not pull the body under.

If the feet are low, raise them by remaining relaxed and *slowly* moving the arms, with the palms up and under water, parallel to the surface of the water to a position over the head. The more the arms are extended in this position the higher the feet will float in the water, because the center of gravity is moved toward the head. Keep the arms under the water at all times.

If you sink, try to hold the proper body position, keeping the lungs

Fig. 8. Back Float with Assistance

full, waiting for the face to return to the surface. The first inclination upon sinking is to struggle to the top. Do not give in; exercise "mind over matter" and hold on and wait for the face to bob up to the surface.

When more air is needed, rapidly exhale and inhale and hold the breath again. If you float well, interchange air slowly and regularly. However, if you tend to sink, interchange air quickly.

Sculling motions (see Fig. 9) at the time of air interchange may be necessary for some persons to remain afloat. Exert a *minimum* (not too much, not too little) amount of downward pressure with your hands. If too much pressure is exerted the head might rise out of water or the legs might be lifted toward the horizontal position; then, when the sculling action is stopped, gravity and momentum working on the legs offset Archimedes' principle of buoyancy. The net result is a feet-first approach to "Davey Jones' locker." Exert just enough pressure to equalize the buoyant effect of the lungs. As soon as the lungs are inflated through inhaling, they serve to buoy up the body and the sculling action can be stopped.

The position of the arms for the sculling action, if needed, is important. To assume the proper position extend the arms underwater out to the side with palms down. Now BEND THE ARMS AT THE ELBOW ONLY so that the fingertips point directly forward; the upper arms are still extended to the side. Now perform the sculling action

Fig. 9. Position and Direction of Minimum Power for Those Who Have Trouble Floating

with pressure exerted downward. REMEMBER—USE ONLY MINIMUM EFFORT.

Now a final word about relaxation when floating. Do NOT BE TENSE OR RIGID. Tensing the muscles requires effort, which in turn uses oxygen, causing air to be needed more often. If the body is stiff, supplemental movements cause it to bob up and down in the water, thus letting momentum and gravity eventually take the body underwater.

Recovering to a standing position from the back float in shallow water is accomplished by simultaneously holding the breath, pulling the knees to the chest, pushing the head *forward*, and scooping the hands down and back and then up. The arm action is like jumping rope backward. Straighten the legs easily until the feet touch bottom. Stand up.

To recover from floating in the vertical position, just lift the head forward and the arms overhead and out of water. The weight of the head and arms out of water increases the force of gravity and causes the feet to go to the bottom.

a

b

Fig. 10. Recovery from Back Float

STEP 5: BEGINNING BACKSTROKE

Ability to swim on the back is essential. Analysis of hundreds of beginning and advanced swimmers reveals that they swim a stroke, especially when tired, which we have chosen to call the beginning backstroke. This stroke is a combination of the backstroke kick and a sculling motion of the hands. Very little effort is required for this stroke and since the face is out of water there is little difficulty with breathing.

Body Position

The basic body position is that of floating horizontally. Keep the ears under water with the water line at the middle of the top of the head. Tuck the chin in, raise the chest up, and allow the hips to bend *slightly*. Extend the legs with the toes pointed and turned inward. Position the arms at the sides with palms down.

Arm Action (Sculling)

Move the hands simultaneously and continuously close to the sides of the body, executing a figure-eight path. Movements of the elbow and shoulder joints assist the action of the hands. Pressure is exerted by the palms downward and toward the feet.

Start with the arms and hands under water extended toward the feet but held about 15 inches away from the body. The angle between the arm and the side of the body at the shoulder joint is about 45 degrees. Cock the wrists. Now, with elbows leading the action, press the water toward the thighs, thumbs up; squeeze the arms inward. When the arms are close to the sides of the body rotate the wrists and forearms inward, still keeping the hands in the cocked position; this action causes the elbow to bend slightly and to point outward. Now press the water away from the body, palms facing downward *and* outward, thumbs down. When the hands return to the starting position rotate the wrists and arms outward, thumbs up; this action causes the elbow to point slightly to the inside. Continue the figure-eight pressing and rotating action, in and down, out and down, always keeping the wrists cocked and the hands under water.

Leg Action

The beginning backstroke leg action is an up-and-down whipping motion of the legs, identical to that of the backstroke. (See page 50 for illustrations of this kick.) On the downward beat allow the leg, which is kept straight, to sink about 8 inches. Then bend the knee in order to allow the foot to reach a depth of approximately 18 inches. Keep the toes pointed and turned in with the ankle joint relaxed. For the upward power action lift the leg, and with a quick straightening of the knee, flip the water in the air with the top of the foot by snapping the ankle joint—just as though you were flipping off a slipper. *The knee remains under water* and the top of the foot just clears the surface of the water. Now allow the straight leg to sink to start the cycle again.

Breathing

Because the face is out of water breathing is no problem. The important thing to remember is to inhale only through the mouth.

Coordination

There is no set rhythm between arms and legs. The beginning backstroke is a resting stroke and is in no way designed for speed. Propulsion occurs as a result of both the arm and leg action, which work simultaneously but independently of one another.

Fig. 11. Sculling Arm Action Used in Beginning Backstroke

STEP 6: POSITION CHANGES

One of the most important skills in learning to be a safe swimmer is the ability to change direction or position in the water. This ability increases the opportunities to develop mobility and endurance.

Turning Around

At first, turn in fairly wide circles; then shorten and sharpen the turns. If you are swimming in the prone position reach slightly toward the new direction during each stroke.

Sculling with only one arm is not very effective for turning around while swimming on your back. Thus a new, single armstroke must be learned for this maneuver. While floating on the back, start with the

Fig. 12. Turning Around While Swimming

arms at the sides. To turn to the right, bend the right elbow and bring the right hand up to the hip. Keeping the arm underwater, slice the hand through the water until the arm is straight and extended to the side at right angles to the body. Now push the water with the hand and forearm toward the feet. When the hand touches the thigh, repeat the complete motion until the body is turned as far as desired. Hold the left arm against the side throughout the turn. Maintain a horizontal position; do *not* let your legs sink.

Turning Over

To turn in a counterclockwise direction from the prone position to the back, reach forward under water with the right arm, keeping the left arm under water at the side. Now turn the head to the left and look back over the left shoulder. At the same time press the water down about six inches with the right palm and forearm; then sweep the right arm in a wide, horizontal circle just under the surface of the water as the body rolls over on to the back. The work of the right arm is important to maintain forward movement and to prevent the feet from sinking. As soon as the back position is reached continue to swim easily or float if desired.

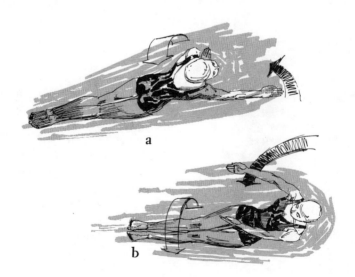

Fig. 13. Turning Over from the Human Stroke to the Beginning Backstroke

To turn counterclockwise from the back to the prone position, start with the arms at the sides, hold the breath, and then turn the shoulders and head to the left. Move the right arm across the front of the body and "step" the right leg over the left leg. Allow the face to submerge as the body turns to the prone position. Immediately proceed to swim and gradually raise the head for air. Keep the feet up by kicking as soon as the prone position is reached.

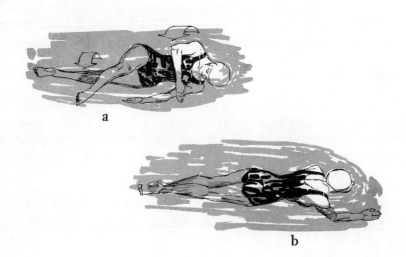

a

b

Fig. 14. Turning Over from the Beginning Backstroke to the Human Stroke

STEP 7: TREADING WATER

The technique of treading water is an important safety skill, which must be mastered before you can be declared a safe swimmer. This technique can be used when you wish to remain in one spot with the head out of water, at such times, for example, as waiting your turn to use a pool ladder. Practice treading water until it can be done for a period of 2–3 minutes without undue fatigue.

Body Position

Maintain a vertical position with the chin just above the surface of the water and with the back straight. Position the arms just under water, extended to the sides of the body, with the legs hanging slightly forward and under the body.

Arm Action

Execute a sculling stroke with the hands (see page 25). Use only minimum effort with pressure exerted downward. Too much effort causes the body to bob up and down, requiring added effort to off-set the force of gravity pulling on the shoulders and chest if they are exposed above the water. Extend the arms to the side and slightly in front of the body about 6–12 inches below the surface. Then use the figure-eight sculling motion with wrists straight and palms down.

Leg Action

Execute an easy, extra-wide, crawl-kick (see page 46). With the legs slightly forward, move them alternately backward and forward using the hip muscles primarily. Keep the ankles and knees loose with toes pointing toward the bottom. Again, do not exert so much effort that the body is lifted too far above the water. Keep the chin at the surface at all times.

Later, after developing skill in executing the sidestroke or breast-stroke (see Chapter 3), the leg action may be modified while treading water. A scissor kick or breaststroke kick may then be used in place of the crawl kick.

Breathing

Since the face is above water there is no breathing problem.

Coordination

There is no set rhythm for the action of the arms and legs. The important thing to remember is that *effort should be minimum*. In fact, as proficiency is developed, treading water may be done by using only the arms or only the legs.

STEP 8: WATER ENTRIES

If you are swimming at a beach you can walk into the water. If you are at a pool you can go down a ladder or slide over the side. However, there are times when you may want to join the gang and jump or dive in, or perhaps need to dive or jump in for safety's sake. Jumping means entering feet first, while most diving is done in an extended, head-down position.

Jumping

When jumping into shallow water (chest-deep), realize that the feet more than likely will touch the bottom. The impact, of course, is lessened because of the resistance of the water and Archimedes' principle of buoyancy. To prevent injury, bend the ankles and knees to cushion the impact.

To jump into deep water start on the deck in a stride position with the toes of one foot gripping the edge of the deck. Step forward with the rear foot and hop with the front foot. Hold the breath and keep the back straight, head up and eyes open. With elbows bent, hold the arms at shoulder level to the outside and slightly forward. Keep the legs bent and in the stride position as the body enters the water to prevent going too deep. Holding the body in a rigid, vertical position causes the body to go straight down.

When returning to the surface after a jump into deep water, move the arms and legs as though you were climbing a ladder. WHEN THE HEAD REACHES THE SURFACE, PUT THE HEAD DOWN, KEEP THE FACE IN THE WATER, AND FORCE THE HIPS UP AND BACK. This action brings the body into the prone position. When the hips reach the surface, start to swim. As soon as you are moving forward then, not before, raise the head for air.

Fig. 15. Jumping into Deep Water and Recovering to the Surface

Diving

Entering the water head first is an aquatic skill to be learned at the same time as learning how to swim. A "head first" dive usually connotes a position with the arms stretched overhead. The actual pattern of water entry is hands, head, and then body. Before describing the techniques for diving, become familiar with the following safety rules:

Know the depth of the water and the presence of obstructions underwater.

Be sure that the water under the diving board is clear of swimmers.

Keep the eyes open to insure safety and to assist in controlling body movement.

There are three steps to follow in learning how to execute a simple standing dive. Experience indicates that DIVING CAN BE LEARNED WITHIN 5 MINUTES if you follow the progressions described below. If at any time difficulty is encountered, return to Step 1 and begin again. Only five minutes of concentrated effort is needed. WHEN FIRST LEARNING HOW TO DIVE, BE SURE TO PRACTICE IN WATER AT LEAST 7 FEET DEEP.

1. *Kneel.* Start by kneeling on one knee with the toes of the other foot curled over the edge of the deck. Extend the arms overhead, interlocking the thumbs and covering the ears with the upper arms. Bend as much as possible from the hips, causing the fingertips to point toward the water at a spot about 3 feet from the side of the pool. Tuck the chin in. Now you are ready to dive. Slowly rock forward on the forward foot by lifting the hips and raising the back knee. As the body overbalances forward continue to raise the back leg and gently push with the forward leg until it is straight. Enter the water at an angle of approximately 45 degrees, about 3 feet from the side of the pool. Do NOT LIFT THE HEAD. Govern the direction of movement under water by raising or lowering the hands through the action of the wrists. The hands serve as a planing surface and direct the movement of the body. If the momentum of the body does not carry you up to the surface, use the "ladder-climbing" action described above (page 33).

2. *Modified stand.* Except for the initial position, all of the actions described in Step 1 above are followed in this progression. In-

stead of kneeling on the back knee, take a short stride position with the toes of one foot curled over the edge of the pool and the foot of the back leg placed on the deck slightly to the side and behind the front foot. Bend both knees slightly. Place the arms and interlock the thumbs as described in Step 1. Be sure to raise the back leg high as the body moves forward.

3. *Stand.* Instead of taking the stride position, as described in Step 2, place both feet together with the toes curled over the edge. Bend the knees slightly, but bend as much as possible from the hips with the arms overhead and thumbs interlocked. As THE BODY OVER-BALANCES FORWARD, THRUST WITH THE FEET AND FORCE THE HIPS AND BOTH LEGS UPWARD, to approximate the lifting action of the back leg described in Steps 1 and 2.

As proficiency is developed, execute the dive without assuming the starting position with the arms overhead before you thrust with the legs. Rather, move the arms from the sides of the body to the proper overhead position as the body moves forward and downward.

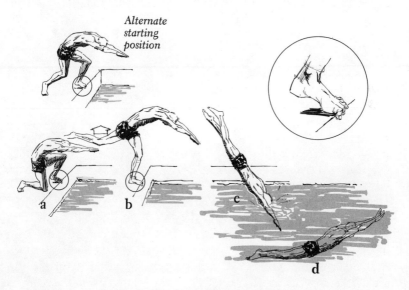

Alternate
starting
position

a   b   c   d

Fig. 16. Diving Progressions

STEP 9: EVALUATION

Evaluating swimming performance is a constant process and is not reserved only for the time after the fundamentals are mastered. Continuous analysis by a qualified instructor throughout the skill development period is the best guide for improvement. To assist in assessing your knowledge and ability, and to provide a measure of incentive, several measuring devices are included at the end of the book. You and your instructor should use the forms provided in Chapter 7 to measure your knowledge, skill and progress.

The more strokes you know, the more enjoyment you can have in the water. Perhaps more important, you will be able to swim longer distances with a repertory of strokes that permits you to rest certain groups of muscles by periodically changing from one stroke to another.

To indicate that there is only one approved method for performing the various strokes would be misleading. First, there is not enough research evidence to document the claim that one form or method is superior to another. Secondly, because of varying body builds, different degrees of strength, different centers of gravity and specific gravity, modifications of form are necessary. This is true particularly of the out-of-water recovery phases of certain strokes as well as of body position.

In the pages to follow, through the use of word pictures and illustrations, six different strokes—elementary backstroke, sidestroke, crawl, backstroke, breaststroke, and butterfly—are analyzed in detail. While reading, try to picture the actions called for and think through each movement.

ELEMENTARY BACKSTROKE

The elementary backstroke is one of the easiest strokes to learn. It can be performed with a minimum amount of energy. Breathing presents little difficulty since the face is out of water. Develop proficiency in this stroke from the start so that you have a stroke to rely upon in case you become tired. Be sure to have clear water ahead since vision is restricted. In particular, be aware of the location of the pool walls so as not to injure your head.

Body Position

Maintaining the body in the correct position is the key to performing this stroke. Lie face up in a horizontal position with the water line at the center of the top of the head with ears underwater. KEEP THE HIPS UP (NEVER LET THEM SAG), CHEST UP, HEAD STEADY WITH

THE CHIN TUCKED IN. The position of the legs varies according to body build.

Arm Action

The action of the arms is continuous from glide to glide. Start with the arms under water with palms flat against the outside of the thighs. KEEPING THE ARMS AND HANDS UNDER WATER AT ALL TIMES, bend the elbows so that they point toward the bottom of the pool and draw the hands to your shoulders. Allow the fingertips to brush against the hips, ribs, and shoulders. The elbows, when completely bent, should point toward the feet and be positioned close to the side of the body. *After* the hands reach the shoulders, extend or straighten the arms, still *under water*, by reaching over the head. Streamline this action by straightening the wrists and slicing the hands through the water. The position of the extended arms, in terms of a clock face, is at "five minutes 'til one." Now catch the water with the hands, fingers extended and together and palms turned outward. Gradually, but quickly, sweep the straight arms in a circular motion to the thighs, allowing the hands to drop no more than about 15 degrees under water. During this sweeping, circular power action, apply pressure to the water with the palms and the inside of the arms. When the hands reach the thighs hold them there for a long resting glide.

Depending upon body buoyancy, the position of the extended arms just prior to the power action may be altered to keep the face above water. Although the ideal position is "five minutes 'til one," this position may be modified to "fifteen minutes 'til three." As you get the feel of the stroke extend the arms to the more desired position. Generally, men need to modify the arm stroke more than women.

Leg Action

The action of the legs is continuous from glide to glide. Start with the legs together under water, toes pointed. Now press the calves of the legs down and bend the ankles and knees (not the hips). Spread the legs slightly and POSITION THE FEET BELOW AND TO THE OUTSIDE OF THE KNEES AND HIPS. This completes the recovery phase of the leg action. To develop power bend the ankles, turn the toes to the outside, circle the feet to the outside and press the water backward and upward with the inside of the feet and legs, allowing the knees to straighten and the legs to squeeze together. Point the toes and hold the legs together for a long resting glide. AT NO TIME DURING THE

LEG ACTION SHOULD ANY PORTION OF THE LEGS AND FEET BE PERMITTED TO RISE ABOVE THE SURFACE OF THE WATER. DO NOT LET THE HIPS BEND OR SAG; if you do, the face is likely to submerge.

Breathing

Each stroke has a definite breathing pattern which contributes to smooth and efficient stroking. If the body is very buoyant, however, the swimmer can breathe at almost any time during the elementary backstroke. The suggested breathing pattern is to inhale and exhale during the glide—breathe out during the beginning of the glide and breathe in toward the end of the glide. The idea is to have the lungs full of air during the recovery phase of the stroke when the body tends to sink.

Coordination

Unlike any other stroke, the elementary backstroke requires simultaneous recovery of the arms and legs and *almost* simultaneous power

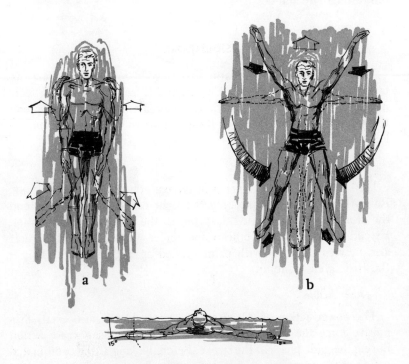

Fig. 17. Elementary Backstroke Coordination

action by both the arms and legs. The timing of the elementary back-stroke is essentially in three counts:

> One: recovery of arms and legs
> Two: power action of arms and legs
> Three: glide—glide—glide

First bend the arms and slice the hands through the water to the "five minutes 'til one" position; at the same time bend the ankles and knees. Second, sweep the arms to the side of the body; at the same time develop power action with the legs. Because the hands take a longer route than the feet, the power action of the legs is completed before finishing the arm power action. Third, after completing the power phase of the arms and legs, rest and *glide* in the position of "attention" allowing the power to thrust the body ahead. When you feel your speed slow down begin the cycle again. Try to cover a distance of 25 yards using only eight or ten complete strokes. Do not stroke too fast. As your strokes become short and choppy, the body tends to bob up and down.

SIDESTROKE

The sidestroke is easily learned. It is good for covering long distances and swimming in rough water, and is basic to life-saving techniques. Note that the instructions below are for those who prefer to swim on the right side. For those who may wish to swim on the left side just interchange the words "left" and "right."

Body Position

Lie on the right side. KEEP THE ENTIRE BODY IN A STRAIGHT LINE. Raise the head slightly, keeping the right ear in the water. Extend the legs with toes pointed just under the surface of the water. Extend the right arm overhead and under water and hold the left arm next to the body with palm pressed against the thigh. This is the basic glide position.

Arm Action

The power action of the arms alternates. As one arm exerts propulsive force the other recovers. However, both arms cease action during the glide phase of the stroke. Before looking at the coordinated action of the arms, let's analyze the action of each arm independently.

Right arm power. Start with the right arm under water and extended over the head. Press the palm down about 10 inches with the arm straight. Now bend the elbow slightly, turn the palm so that it faces the feet and PRESS THE WATER BACK TOWARD THE FEET WITH PALM AND FOREARM. Stop this press when the forearm is directly under the chest. This completes the power action.

Right arm recovery. Squeeze the elbow into the side of the body, keeping the elbow bent. Gently bring the forearm to a position pointing toward the direction of travel. Straighten the arm and SLICE THE HAND FORWARD THROUGH THE WATER until the arm is extended to the starting position. Now GLIDE BY STRETCHING FORWARD WITHOUT PRESSING DOWN.

Left arm recovery. Start with the left arm next to the body with the palm pressed down and flat against the thigh. KEEPING THE HAND AND ELBOW UNDER WATER AND AS CLOSE TO THE BODY AS POSSIBLE, bend the elbow and bring the hand under the right cheek, palm down. Be sure to streamline this negative movement.

Left arm power. WITH THE HAND AND FOREARM, PUSH THE WATER DOWN AND BACK TOWARD THE FEET by straightening the arm. When the hand reaches the thigh, stop action and glide.

Arm coordination. The work of both arms is coordinated in three counts:

> One: right arm power, left arm recovery
> Two: left arm power, right arm recovery
> Three: glide—glide—glide

Other ways of thinking about the coordinated arm action are, "Bend—Extend—Glide," or "Press right—Push left—Glide."

Leg Action

The action of the legs in the sidestroke is called the scissor kick, because the power action of the legs is much the same as the closing action of a pair of scissors. Start with the legs extended and together, toes pointed. Draw the knees toward the chest and the heels toward the hips until the angle at the hip joint between thigh and abdomen is approximately 90 degrees. The left knee is several inches closer to the chest than the right knee. Bend the left ankle. KEEPING KNEES BENT AND THE LEGS HORIZONTAL AND PARALLEL, reach the right foot as far behind the body as possible; at the same time reach the left

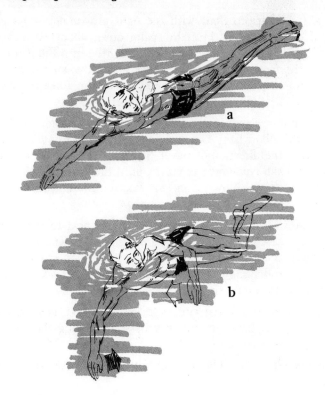

Fig. 18. Sidestroke Coordination

foot as far in front of the body as possible. Do NOT ALLOW THE RIGHT KNEE TO SINK BELOW THE HORIZONTAL PLANE OF THE ENTIRE RIGHT LEG. Sweep both legs in as wide an arc as possible, bringing them together as though you were closing a pair of scissors. Exert pressure against the water with the bottom of the left foot and the back of the left leg, and with the top of the right foot and front of the right leg. When the legs come together stop all effort, point the toes and glide. Do NOT LET THE LEGS PASS EACH OTHER.

Breathing

The coordination of breathing with the timing of the stroke is simple. Inhale during the "bending" phase, as the right arm exerts power; exhale during the glide.

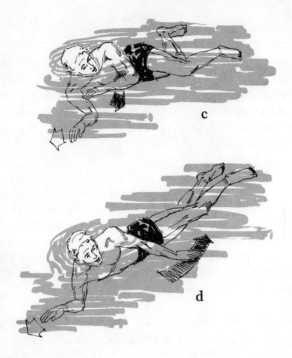

c

d

Coordination

The timing of the arms and legs is three counts:

One: Bend—bend right arm in power action, bend left arm in recovery phase, and bend legs in recovery action.

Two: Extend—extend right arm in recovery phase, extend left arm in power action, and extend legs in scissor-power action; terminate all three of these actions simultaneously.

Three: Glide—glide and rest on your side until your speed slows down; then start the cycle again.

As with the elementary backstroke, try to swim a distance of 25 yards using approximately eight or ten complete strokes.

CRAWL

The crawl is the fastest stroke devised by man to date. It is one of the most popular strokes in America and one with which you should be familiar. It is used to move rapidly from one spot to another and when thoroughly learned is used to swim long distances. Although the crawl is not very easy to learn, it can become a relaxing stroke when executed properly and is worth the time required to learn it well.

Body Position

Assume a horizontal prone position. Keep the head, hips, and heels (3 H's) at the surface of the water to promote streamlining and to minimize water turbulence. Submerge the face so that the surface of the water is approximately at the hairline on the forehead. Hold the chin forward away from the neck except when turning for a breath. RELAX THE NECK MUSCLES. Keep the eyes open. Hunch the shoulders forward, especially as speed is increased. KEEP THE HIPS UP. If the hips sag the streamlining of the body is lessened. Perhaps more important, when the hips sink the action of the buttock muscles in kicking and the back muscles in arm stroking is impaired. Sagging hips also interfere with deep breathing. Hold the legs loosely in an extended position, with toes pointed and turned in.

Arm Action

Move the arms so that as one arm exerts power under water, the other arm is recovering over the water. The underwater action of the arms is, of course, most important to propulsion. Analysis of champion swimmers indicates that THE ARMS SHOULD MOVE UNDER WATER WITH THE ELBOWS BENT, pressing the water down and then pushing the water back so that a swirl of water is thrust between the thighs.

Start with the arm extended over the head and under water with the FINGERS TOGETHER and with the HAND SLIGHTLY CUPPED. Place the hand so that it rests on the extension of the mid-line of the body running from head to toe. "Catch" the water before applying too much pressure. (See Fig. 19, page 47.) The catch is like "taking hold" of an object before it is lifted. *Feel* the water pressure with the palm and gradually, yet quickly, develop power. Without a gradual development of power the hand and arm tend to slip out of the path of maximum water resistance. This results in either decreased power or wasted energy. See page 9 for an explanation of this principle.

Now with an increasing amount of power, press the hand down about six inches, BEND THE ELBOW ABOUT 45 DEGREES and push the water back with the palm of the hand and the underside of the forearm. KEEP THE HAND ALONG THE MID-LINE OF YOUR BODY until it passes about 45 degrees beyond a vertical position. In other words, pressure is exerted through a downward, front-to-back arc of about 135 degrees; however most of the power comes during the last 90 degrees of the arc.

Throughout the underwater power action of the arms be conscious of using the muscles of the upper back as well as of the torso to assist the arms. This is accomplished primarily by two conditions. First, maintaining the proper body position brings the weight and muscles of the torso into action. Don't let the shoulders move too far forward by overreaching. Second, the alternate action of the other arm assists in developing maximum power.

At the completion of the underwater power action of the arm THE MUSCLES CONTROLLING THE ACTION OF THE SHOULDER JOINT TAKE OVER THE RECOVERY, while the back and arm muscles are relatively relaxed. Momentum from the power action assists the shoulder-joint muscles in the recovery phase of the arm stroke. During the recovery BEND THE ELBOW, RAISING THE ARM OUT OF THE WATER. Move the hand forward in a slight circling action to the outside, keeping the elbow higher than the wrist. The fingertips should just clear the water. As the upper arm moves forward allow it to come near to the ear.

After the shoulder-joint muscles throw the arm forward, they too partially relax and momentum and gravity assist in getting the arm back into the water. SLIDE THE ARM INTO THE WATER DIRECTLY IN FRONT OF THE SHOULDER, WITH THE HAND ENTERING THE WATER FIRST. Upon entry into the water ride or glide the hand and arm forward, or begin the underwater power action immediately. If speed is not desired, the glide is recommended. Be sure that the hand and arm glide in a streamlined position; don't push the hand forward and create negative movement. If speed is desired, reduce the length of the glide or eliminate it completely. Be sure, however, to catch the water before applying maximum power action.

Ideally, the swimmer should exert continuous effort with the arms—first one, then the other, so as not to have a pulsating or jerky forward movement. By keeping the arm action constant inertia does not have to be overcome. Thus as one arm applies power the other recovers and "rests" from the end of the power action to the beginning of a new power action.

Leg Action

The commonly executed leg action is the up-and-down, whip-like motion coordinated so that there are either four or six beats to a complete arm cycle (or two or three beats for the power action of each arm). This crawl kick is identical to the kick learned for the human stroke. See page 21 for a complete discussion of the proper kicking action.

Breathing

Normally there is one breathing cycle for each complete arm cycle. Starting with the face in the water with the nose straight down and chin held away from the neck, exhale through the mouth or nose and mouth. As the right arm passes through the vertical during the power phase of the stroke turn the head to the right about 60 degrees so that the face is out of water; then QUICKLY INHALE THROUGH THE UPPER CORNER OF THE MOUTH. Complete the inhalation and RETURN THE FACE TO THE WATER JUST AFTER THE START OF THE POWER ACTION OF THE LEFT ARM AND JUST AS THE RIGHT ELBOW IS AT ITS HIGHEST POINT DURING THE RECOVERY ACTION OF THE RIGHT ARM. Avoid turning the head to the right *just* as the left arm enters the water; this causes a jerky, lunging action. Learn how to breathe when turning the head to either the right or left. This allows you a wider range of vision and helps to relax the neck muscles.

Coordination

ALLOW THE LEGS TO WORK EASILY INTO RHYTHM WITH THE ARMS. Do not allow the arms and legs to work independently of each other, since total body balance is upset and power is lost. The proper rhythm might be explained best by the phrases, "RIGHT ARM IN, RIGHT LEG UP; LEFT ARM IN, LEFT LEG UP." In other words as the right arm enters the water the right leg kicks up (first beat), and when the left arm enters the water the left leg kicks up (fourth beat). There is a total of six beats—three upward motions of each leg—to a complete arm cycle. The series of six drawings illustrates the correct arm-leg-breathing coordination.

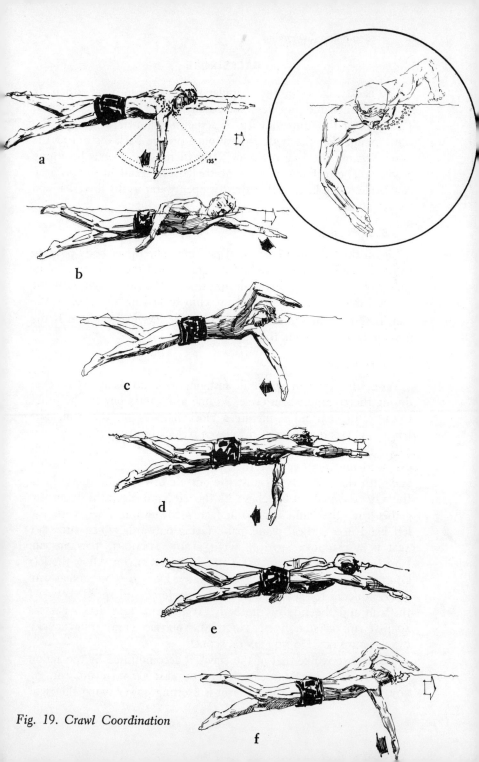

Fig. 19. Crawl Coordination

BACKSTROKE

The backstroke is another popular stroke used in competition. It is easily learned and provides a means for moving rapidly on the back. The work of the arms and legs is *somewhat* similar to that of the crawl except that the body is positioned on the back instead of the front. Because the face is out of water there is no serious breathing problem. The fact that vision is restricted can result in serious accidents. Therefore be sure that there is open water in the direction you are traveling.

Body Position

Lie on the back in a horizontal position. The upper body position varies, depending upon your specific gravity and the location of your center of gravity. In general, however, keep the head high with the ears just out of the water, chest up, chin tucked in, and eyes on the feet. Lower the hips slightly and extend the legs under water. If the hips are bent too much, the body will be too low.

Arm Action

Work the arms in windmill fashion, with no delay whatsoever during the complete arm cycle. As one arm exerts power, the other recovers. In your mind picture a clock hanging on the wall. The left arm enters the water at the eleven o'clock position; the right arm enters the water at the one o'clock position. Start with the left arm extended under water over the head in the eleven o'clock position and with the right arm against the outside of the right thigh. Press the water down about 6 inches with the left hand. Keep the fingers together with the hand flat, palm facing downward. Then with the left hand in a vertical plane, palm facing outward, SWEEP THE LEFT ARM IN A CIRCULAR MOTION, WITH ELBOW STRAIGHT, TOWARD THE FEET, ALWAYS KEEPING THE PALM IN A VERTICAL PLANE. Allow the left arm to sink several inches below the water. Do NOT SCOOP UNDER THE BODY. Squeeze the water, with increasing force and speed, between the arm and the side of the body. WHEN THE LEFT HAND PRESSES AGAINST THE OUTSIDE OF THE THIGH IMMEDIATELY START ITS RECOVERY OVER THE WATER. Do NOT FIN OR SCULL!

The recovery, like that of the crawl, is accomplished by the action of the shoulder-joint muscles. KEEP THE ARM RELAXED AND THE ELBOW STRAIGHT. While the left arm is exerting power swing the right

arm upwards, outwards, and back to the one o'clock position. DUR-
ING THE RECOVERY ALLOW THE RELAXED HAND TO PASS OVER THE WATER
TO THE SIDE AND NOT DIRECTLY ABOVE THE BODY. The hand, in effect,
follows the outline of an elongated parabola as it moves throughout
the entire stroke. Toward the end of the recovery allow the shoulder
muscles to relax and let momentum and gravity carry the right arm
to the one o'clock entry position. At the end of the recovery slide
the right hand into the water with the fingers (little finger first)
entering first. Then press and catch the water and immediately begin
the power action as described for the left arm in the paragraph immediately above.

Remember that the arms work in direct opposition to each other,
180 degrees out of phase. The action of one arm aids the action of the
other, bringing into play the strong upper back muscles and keeping
the body balanced. During the work of the arms do not let the body
sway from side to side. Two actions prevent body sway. First, hold
the head steady, keeping the eyes looking toward the feet. Second,
place the hands in the water at the five minutes 'til one position. Do
not reach toward the twelve o'clock position.

Leg Action

The alternating, up-and-down whipping action of the leg drive in
the backstroke is very important. Without sufficient leg power too
much strain is placed upon the arms, causing early tiredness. The backstroke kick is identical to the kick learned for the beginning
backstroke. See page 27 for a complete discussion of the proper
kicking action.

Breathing

Because the face is out of water breathing is not a serious problem.
However, try to keep the breathing cycle regular and in rhythm with
the arm stroke. It is best to exhale during the power action of one of
the arms.

Coordination

To get maximum power there must be total body balance. This
comes from a proper timing of the arms and legs. Generally most
champions use a six-beat kicking action—that is, three beats for each
arm or six beats for a complete arm cycle. The proper rhythm can be
remembered by the phrase, "RIGHT HAND IN, LEFT LEG UP; LEFT HAND
IN, RIGHT LEG UP." As the right hand enters the water the left leg

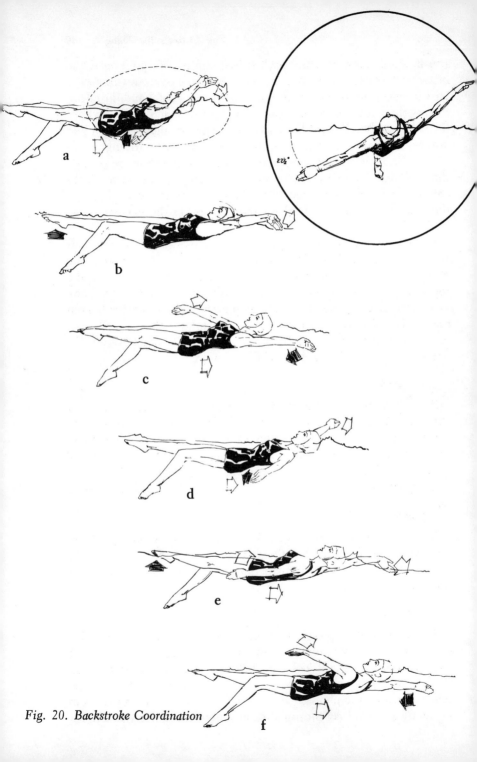

Fig. 20. *Backstroke Coordination*

exerts upward force. Note that the backstroke arm-leg coordination is opposite to the crawl arm-leg coordination.

To establish the proper arm-leg coordination, ALLOW THE LEGS TO FIT AUTOMATICALLY TO THE ARMS. When the proper rhythm is felt the first and fourth beats should be accentuated—that is, the upward power action of the legs at the moment the opposite hand enters the water should be more forceful. Try saying to yourself, "*One*, two, three; *four*, five, six" with the hands entering the water on counts *one* and *four*.

BREASTSTROKE

The breaststroke is one of the oldest strokes and is used in competition. Once the difficult coordination of the breaststroke is mastered, the stroke can be used for swimming long distances and in rough water.

Body Position

Unlike all of the other strokes, the breaststroke requires varying prone body positions. During the glide the body is flat on the surface of the water; when inhaling, the body is on a slight downward angle with the head slightly higher than the feet.

Arm Action

The arms offer very little propulsive power. Use them primarily to support the lifting of the head to get air. The action of the arms is continuous from glide to glide. The hands describe a heart-shaped path. With the arms extended in front of the body,

Fig. 21.   *Heart-shaped Path of Breaststroke Arm Action*

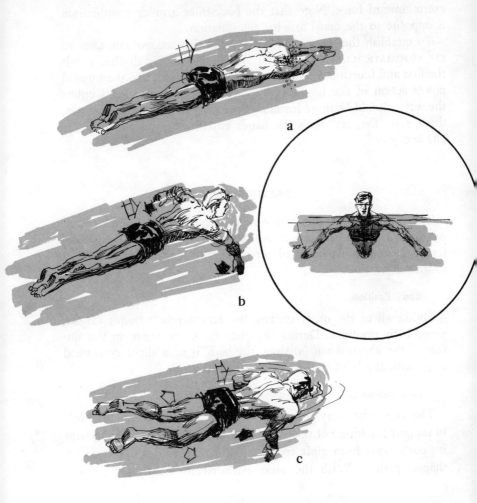

Fig. 22. Breaststroke Coordination

thumbs touching, palms down, fingers together, press the water simultaneously with both hands and forearms in a combined down-ward, outward and backward motion. DURING THE PRESS, BEND THE ELBOWS. At the same time, hunch the shoulders forward, raise the head slightly, and thrust the chin forward. At this point, inhale. Stop the press when the fingertips and lower forearms are pointing straight down. Then squeeze the upper arms into the sides of the

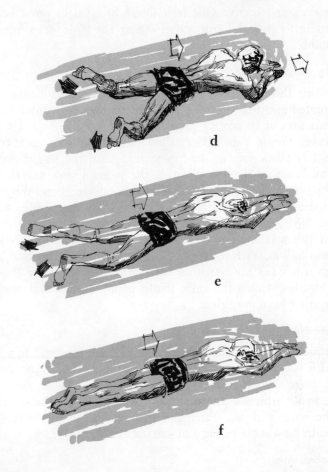

d

e

f

body and bring the hands together under the chest. Never let the hands go past an imaginary line even with the shoulders. At the same time lower the head into the water. Now thrust the arms and hands forward to the starting position, trying to streamline them against negative resistance. HOLD THE ARMS OUTSTRETCHED UNDER WATER AND EXHALE. THIS HOLDING PHASE OF THE ARM STROKE IS ESSENTIAL IN ORDER TO TAKE ADVANTAGE OF THE GLIDE RESULTING FROM

A POWERFUL LEG ACTION. One technique which might prove helpful in learning to stop the arm action during the glide is to interlock the thumbs.

Leg Action

To learn this kick start with the legs outstretched behind you, toes pointed and feet together. Keeping the hips horizontal (NEVER PRESS THE HIPS UP OR DOWN), press the thighs down and quickly draw both knees toward (not under) the chest, forming an angle of approximately 60 degrees at the hip joint. Spread the legs slightly as hips and knees are bent, and MOVE THE HEELS UNDER WATER TO A POSITION OUTSIDE OF THE KNEES AND HIPS. Rotate and bend the ankles so that the toes are drawn toward the knees and are pointed to the outside. Now you are ready for the power action. APPLY PRESSURE AGAINST THE WATER WITH THE INSTEPS AND INNER PART OF THE SHINS BY PUSHING THE LEGS OUTWARD AND SLIGHTLY DOWNWARD; THEN SQUEEZE THE LEGS TOGETHER AS THEY STRAIGHTEN. When the feet come together stretch the ankle joints, point the toes and hold the legs together for a *long* glide.

Breathing

The breathing cycle is simple yet exact. Raise the head to a position with the chin on the water and INHALE THROUGH THE MOUTH DURING (NOT BEFORE, NOT AFTER) THE POWER ACTION OF THE ARMS. As the upper arms are squeezed into the sides, lower the face back into the water with the water line at the center of the head. Hold the breath for a short period and EXHALE DURING THE GLIDE.

Coordination

The timing of the arm and leg action in the breaststroke also is exact. Unless pressure is applied at the correct instant, inertia will have to be overcome. Learn to feel or sense when the movement through the water is slowing down, for at this instant the glide must be terminated and the stroke cycle started again.

The timing might best be described as a four-count coordination:

> One: Power action with the arms (inhale)
> Two: Recover the legs as the hands move under the chin
> Three: Power action with the legs as the arms streamline
>   to the glide position.
> Four: Glide—glide—glide (exhale)

Overcoming faulty stroke-timing habits in the breaststroke is extremely difficult. It is easier to learn the correct timing from the start. Avoid practicing the wrong timing.

BUTTERFLY

The butterfly, the only American stroke, developed by David A. Armbruster, former swimming coach at the University of Iowa, has become an increasingly popular stroke. The stroke receives its name from the arm recovery action, wherein both arms are simultaneously recovered over the water. To execute the butterfly properly requires sophisticated timing of the arm and leg action and considerable stamina to swim it for any distance.

Body Position

Although the basic body position is prone, the alignment of the body along the horizontal varies due to a natural, porpoise-like, undulating movement caused by the synchronized arm and leg action.

Arm Action

Start with the arms extended over the head and under water with the hands several inches apart, palms slightly cupped and facing down. Moving the arms simultaneously, press the water down and to the outside until the hands are positioned just outside of a line extending forward from the shoulders and 8–10 inches below the surface of the water. Turn the palms inward and continue to apply power backward toward the mid-line of the body. Concentrate on moving the torso up and over the hands as pressure is directed backward and *slightly* inward toward the thighs. Apply pressure with the palms and underside of the forearms with the elbows bent about 45 degrees as in the crawl arm power action. Continue this power action until the hands pass about 45 degrees beyond a vertical position, as in the crawl armstroke. At this point push water with the palms toward the feet by straightening the elbows until the hands reach the outside of the thighs. This completes the arm power action.

To recover the arms relax the back and arm muscles, letting momentum from the power action assist the shoulder-joint muscles. Raise the arms out of the water, upper arm first, and circle the hands outward and forward with the wrists loose and the back of the hands facing upward and forward. During the recovery the elbow is straight, yet relaxed, and the fingertips just clear the surface of the water.

After the shoulder-joint muscles throw the arms forward in a horizontal plane, they too should be relaxed allowing momentum and gravity to assist in getting the arms back into the water at a position just outside of the shoulders. When the arms reach a forward position of "five minutes 'til one," slide them inward into the water. Allow the head and shoulders to porpoise, or dive forward and *slightly* downward, as the arms move inward to the starting position for the power action.

Leg Action

A simultaneous up-and-down whip-like action of the legs constitutes the dolphin or fish-tail kick utilized in the butterfly. This action is similar to the crawl kick except that both legs work together instead of alternately, with only two beats to a complete arm stroke instead of three beats. It is the simultaneous motion of the legs that causes the entire body to undulate. In executing the dolphin kick concentrate on flexing and extending the knees, rather than on any hip action. Experience indicates that focusing attention on the hip action reduces the effectiveness of the leg power action.

Start with the legs extended under water behind the body, toes pointed and feet turned slightly inward, knees bent about 30 degrees. With the top of the feet gently press the water down and back and then quickly straighten the knees, which motion whips the feet downward. Now lift both legs upward from the hips, allowing the knees to bend toward the end of the upward movement. At the end of the upward movement the knees again are bent 30 degrees. Repeat the downward, whip-like power action. AT NO TIME SHOULD THE FEET BE RAISED ABOVE THE WATER.

Breathing

Normally there is one breathing cycle for each complete arm cycle. However, in competition, swimmers breathe during every second or third arm stroke in order to keep the body more streamlined and to eliminate effort expended to raise the head out of water. Inhale during the arm recovery action when the hands leave the water during the recovery. Concentrate on pushing the head forward during inhalation, rather than raising the chin upwards, in order to

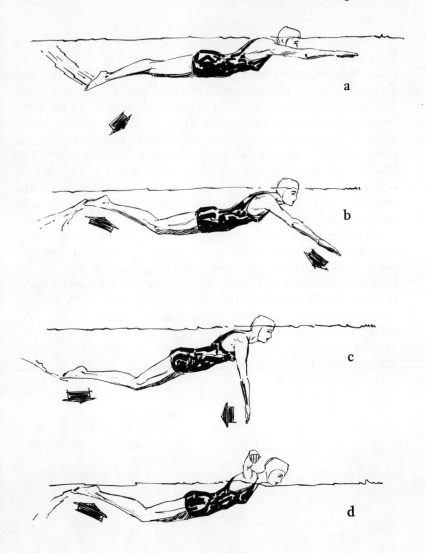

Fig. 23. Butterfly Coordination

prevent lifting the upper torso out of the water. Exhale forcibly during the arm power action when the arms are pressing through the vertical plane.

Coordination

A two-beat kick for each arm stroke advocated here seems to be the easiest arm-leg coordination to learn and execute, although some competitive swimmers use a three-beat rhythm. The proper two-beat rhythm might best be remembered by the phrase "arms in, legs down; arms press, legs down." This means that as the arms enter the water following the recovery, the legs are whipping downward (first beat); as the arms are exerting their maximum power (through the vertical plane) the legs again are whipping downward (second beat). The resulting action is a syncopated rhythm with a shorter and quicker leg action on the first beat and a slight pause or hesitancy during the arm recovery. This pause occurs at the end of the whipping action of the second leg action.

Allow the legs to work easily into rhythm with the arms. Uncoordinated arm-leg action destroys total body balance and dissipates power. Concentrate on the down-beat of the leg action just as the arms enter the water and just as the arms are pressing directly under the body. Don't accentuate the kick. It will fit in normally without overconcentration. Too many persons, just beginning to learn the butterfly, work too hard at the arm-leg rhythm.

WATERMANSHIP TECHNIQUES 4

There is a difference between merely swimming and being at home in the water. A swimmer who is not upset by any circumstance that may occur, who can swim a considerable distance, can remain in the water for a long period of time, can swim under water, and knows when and how to assist others is completely safe—at home—in the water. He has conquered a new medium which he controls for *his* purposes. He does not let the water control him. Such a swimmer has *watermanship*.

Watermanship is a term being popularized through survival swimming and "drownproofing" techniques. This may sound ominous but watermanship skills make up your personal insurance policy in swimming. Children learn to be at home in the water indirectly through the games they play naturally and through many hours of just "fooling around" in the water. Follow-the-leader, diving for objects, and stay-under-the-water contests provide opportunities to accept the unexpected in swimming and to handle each situation as it arises. Adults, however, acquire watermanship by concentrating on learning specific skills.

PERSONAL SAFETY SKILLS

The following safety techniques provide a basis for learning to be completely at home in the water. These skills are "drownproofing," underwater swimming, progressive bobbing and surface diving.

Drownproofing

Professor Fred Lanoue of Georgia Institute of Technology has developed a technique which he calls *drownproofing*. Properly executed, THIS TECHNIQUE REQUIRES AN ABSOLUTE MINIMUM OF ENERGY to stay alive in the water for an extended period of time. This method also can be used when swimming fully clothed, injured, or in rough water. To be sure, drownproofing is not a fancy stroke, but you can learn it on your own and be able to *stay afloat for hours*. Follow the steps described below:

1. Start with the lungs full of air, floating in a vertical position, face down, with the back of the neck at the surface of the water and with the arms and legs hanging down.

2. Keeping the back and face in the same position as Step 1, get ready (recover) for a downward arm and leg power action. Do this by *slowly* moving the arms to a position just under water in front of the head, with the elbows bent; at the same time *slowly* recover the legs for a downward scissor kick.

3. Gently press the arms outward, just under the surface, to a position in front of the shoulders. The arm position is identical to that of treading water. AT THE SAME TIME EXHALE WHILE (NOT BEFORE, NOT AFTER) RAISING THE HEAD OUT OF WATER TO A VERTICAL POSITION, with the chin at the surface of the water.

4. Now inhale and press the arms *downward*, as in the underwater breaststroke (see page 62), and execute a downward scissor kick. Apply just enough power with the arms and legs to keep only the head above water. Do not lift the shoulders above the surface.

5. As the body submerges, *immediately* recover the arms and legs and simultaneously execute a second arm and leg action, *downward and backward*. This action moves the body upward and forward to the surface, returning it to the beginning vertical position. Exert only enough power to bring the body to the surface.

6. Hold the breath and *relax* while floating with the arms and legs hanging down, as in Step 1. Rest for a period of 3–10 seconds. Then begin the cycle again.

Because of their buoyancy, some persons, particularly girls and women, will need to exert only a minimum amount of force with the arms and legs in Steps 4 and 5. However, the complete sequence should be learned by all persons in order to be prepared for emergency situations when cast into the water fully clothed.

As proficiency is developed experiment with holding the hands behind the back and using only leg power action during Steps 4 and 5. Also try this technique by crossing the legs "Buddha-style" and use only arm power action. Tests indicate that if this technique can be performed using either arms or legs alone for 10 minutes, it can be done for an hour or more.

Fig. 24. Drownproofing Steps

Underwater Swimming

If you wish to participate in skin and SCUBA diving (see Glossary), synchronized swimming, and certain other water sports you must be able to swim under water. The capacity to hold the breath is a prerequisite for executing this skill. Two of the most commonly used underwater swimming strokes are a modified dog paddle and the underwater breaststroke.

Modified dog paddle. Except for lengthening the arm stroke and lowering the head, the modified dog paddle (under water) is identical to the human stroke (see Chapter 2). Instead of applying arm power under the head and chest, extend the arm completely forward with the elbow straight and then apply power with the cupped hand and forearm. Sweep the arm, as in the human stroke, backward under the body to the thigh. Then streamline the recovery as in the human stroke.

Employ the up-and-down, whip-like kick of the human stroke while swimming under water; however, allow the legs to move through a greater vertical arc. Utilize the same arm-leg coordination of the human stroke. Rubber flippers or fins may be used to increase speed.

Some swimmers used the modified dog paddle (under water) while positioned on their side. The arm and leg actions then work in horizontal rather than vertical planes.

Underwater breaststroke. The underwater breaststroke is very powerful and takes less energy to execute than the modified underwater dog paddle. ALTHOUGH THE LEG ACTION IS IDENTICAL TO THE CONVENTIONAL BREASTSTROKE, THE ARM ACTION AND ARM-LEG COORDINATION ARE ENTIRELY DIFFERENT.

Body position: Many beginners have difficulty remaining under water. The head (and shoulder) position is the key to staying under the surface. Hold the body under water in a horizontal plane with hips *slightly* raised. Keep the chin tucked in at all times. During the glide keep the shoulders rounded, arms at the sides, palms *up*. Let the legs trail, feet together and toes pointed.

Arm action: Start with the arms extended overhead and directly forward, fingers together and palms down, with the upper arms covering the ears, chin tucked in. Simultaneously press the hands outward and downward to a position directly forward and slightly to the outside of the shoulders. Keeping the forearms in a vertical plane (by moving the elbows in) start the power action by pressing the

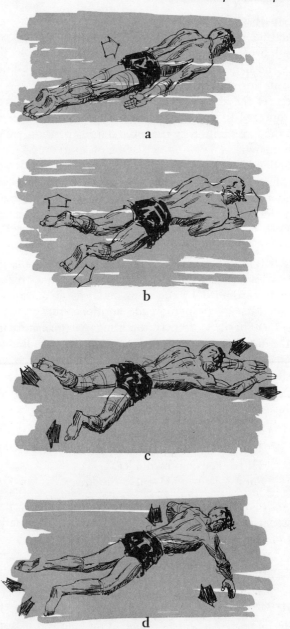

Fig. 25. *Underwater Swimming Coordination*

upper arms back toward the feet, causing the elbows to bend. At the same time cock the wrists. Now vigorously apply pressure downward and backward with the elbows leading, sharply flexing the wrists as the hands move to the side of the thighs. Glide and rest the arms in this position, with palms *up*.

To recover the arms, bring the hands up to the chin, keeping the elbows squeezed to the sides. Then slice your hands directly forward through the water until they reach the starting position. IMMEDIATELY BEGIN THE POWER ACTION; DO NOT GLIDE OR HESITATE.

Leg action: Employ the breaststroke kick described on page 54.

Breathing: Before submerging take two or three deep breaths, exhaling as much as possible and inhaling deeply just before going under water. Periodic, slight exhalations while under water may help you to stay under water. When you feel a distinct tightness in your chest, return to the surface.

Coordination: The timing of the arms and legs in the underwater breaststroke is similar to that of the elementary backstroke (see page 39). Power is applied by the arms and legs at approximately the same time. Starting from the glide position, arms at the sides and legs together, begin to recover the arms. As the hands move from under the head to the extended position, recover the legs. Then apply power with the arms and legs. Complete the arm power action shortly after completing the leg power action. Now glide with the chin tucked in and relax. When forward momentum stops begin the cycle again. The proper timing is in four counts:

> One: Begin arm recovery
> Two: Recover legs and complete arm recovery
> Three: Power arms and legs
> Four: Glide—glide—glide—and relax

Caution. To prevent injury be sure to open the eyes and maintain a visual point of reference, such as a tiled lane marker on the bottom of the pool. Although you must "make up your mind" to hold the breath for a long period of time, don't over-extend yourself; fainting may result.

Progressive Bobbing

The technique of repeatedly bobbing up and down from the surface to the bottom and moving forward in a horizontal direction was developed for use by landing forces during World War II. Because

Fig. 26. Progressive Bobbing

troops were fully clothed and carried equipment it was impossible for them to swim. However, by bobbing in water 10–12 feet in depth, troops were able to reach shallow water safely. This technique also is useful for ordinary persons who find themselves cast overboard from a fishing boat fully clothed in water not more than 10–12 feet deep.

To learn this skill start by treading water in water about 9–10 feet deep. Simultaneously execute a vigorous scissor or breaststroke kick and a downward arm press. After the torso is lifted out of the water, press the water up as you move the arms to a position out of the water and directly overhead. Inhale. Since gravity works on those portions of the body out of the water, the higher the body is lifted out of the water the better. As the body moves directly downward point the toes, keep the arms overhead, and streamline the body as much as possible. If necessary, scull with the hands overhead if the effect of gravity and momentum do not force the body to the bottom.

Upon reaching the bottom, bend the knees and bring the hands under the chin with the elbows close to the sides. Now lean forward and extend the arms overhead as the legs push from the bottom at a 45-degree angle forward and upward. As the body begins to decelerate exert a vigorous arm stroke, using the motion described for the arm action of the underwater breaststroke (see page 62), directed slightly sideward but primarily downward and backward. Continue to glide upward and forward with the hands at the sides.

As the head breaks the surface of the water exhale and slowly draw the knees toward the chest bringing the back to a vertical position. Then repeat the arm and leg action as in the beginning. Continue to bob up and down, gradually moving forward. It is possible to cover a distance of 30–40 feet using three or four thrusts from the bottom.

Surface Diving

During a surface dive the body moves from the surface to a position under water. Know how to surface dive before trying skin and SCUBA diving, synchronized swimming, and life saving. Surface dives are performed either feet first or head first.

Feet first. When not sure of conditions at the bottom or when a quick descent is necessary use the feet-first method. The feet-first maneuver is identical to the first three steps of progressive bobbing (see page 64). When completely submerged draw the knees to the chest, thrust the head forward and roll into a prone position to swim under water. Return to the surface when more air is needed.

Head first. Start by developing considerable forward momentum, using the breaststroke. When ready to submerge inhale, lower the head and press the arms back to the sides, using a breaststroke-like arm action. During the arm action, bend forward from the hips. When the hands reach the sides of the body turn the palms forward. Now vigorously snap the legs up and back out of the water, knees straight; at the same time scoop water upward with the hands and forearms. The body is now in an upside-down position with the arms extended "above" the head toward the bottom of the pool. Allow momentum and gravity to pull the body under as far as possible. If the surface dive is properly executed a depth of 10 or 12 feet can be

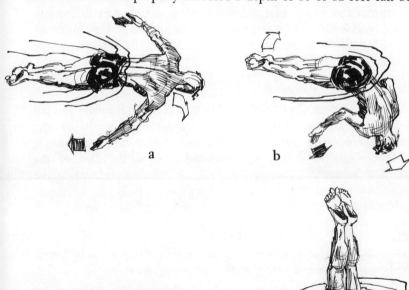

Fig. 27. Surface Diving

reached without any additional arm or leg action. If necessary use one of the underwater swimming strokes to move to any desired location. If greater depth is desired go into the surface dive with the knees and hips bent. Execute a half forward tuck somersault and, when the head is pointed to the bottom of the pool, extend the legs upward and the body drops as described above.

PREVENTING WATER EMERGENCIES

Personal and group safety around water is everyone's concern and is an essential part of every aquatic program. It is important for everyone to know how to prevent aquatic emergencies, how to offer rescue assistance and how to render first aid.

Common Sense Rules

Situations which require aid or help should never happen. The sad fact that they do occur and result in tragic accidents emphasizes the need for preventive water-safety education. Following a few simple common sense rules will prevent most emergencies. One of the deterring factors to following these rules is their simplicity. It is the mature individual who recognizes the gravity of aquatic situations and insists that rules be followed.

Swim only in an adequately supervised area.

Know the water in which you swim. Inquire about such factors as the type of bottom, depth of water and diving areas.

Swim only in areas which are suitable for your ability. When swimming a long distance, save enough energy to return.

Have a clean bill of health for swimming.

Observe all hygienic principles and health rules.

Obey all rules of good conduct and consideration.

Learn thoroughly the survival techniques of "drownproofing," progressive bobbing, and underwater swimming.

Participate in boating activities according to your swimming ability.

In case of an emergency, stay cool, think calmly, and conserve your energy. Don't panic.

Emergency Assistance

When emergencies do arise there are certain ways in which a non-swimmer or beginning swimmer can be very helpful. Always keep in mind that you should not create a second emergency. It is folly to place your life in jeopardy in addition to those already involved. The first thing to do is to stay calm and appraise the situation. Ask yourself the following questions: "To what extent is the person in danger? Is qualified help available? What is nearby to provide a means of rescue or assistance?" If possible, go for help. This is the most important thing you can do. If no help is available, look for a flotation or reaching device to assist the person in difficulty. Try to have a calming influence on him. Talk to him, tell him help is coming, and encourage him to conserve his energy.

On-shore rescue. Reaching poles are the safest, easiest, and most effective means of assistance by a person not proficient in life-saving skills. Any pole or long, rigid item will do. If there is nothing around which can be used to reach the victim, look for a flotation device such as a plank—anything which will act as a means of temporary support. Do not throw such a piece of equipment in the water since its rebound may be uncontrollable. Slide the object along the surface of the water in the direction of the person in difficulty. Perhaps a piece of rope can be found which will be suitable for throwing. After the victim has grasped the rope, draw him in carefully, being sure not to lose your balance.

First aid. Following a rescue, the application of standard first aid is essential. Thus you should be skilled at applying artificial respiration, stopping bleeding, and treating for shock. The American National Red Cross provides free courses of instruction in first aid. Avail yourself of this opportunity and be ready to do your part following a water emergency.

THE WONDERFUL WORLD
OF WATER SPORTS

5

The wonderful world of water sports is made up of many exciting and fun-filled activities. A number of these sports are briefly described below to give you an introduction to aquatics. These sports require varying amounts of swimming ability and it is essential that you explore these activities under competent supervision. The Bibliography at the end of the book may be consulted for additional information about each sport.

Swimming and Diving

To become a proficient swimmer with endurance and ability to execute many strokes takes time. Springboard diving is another activity in which time and intelligent practice are essential. Your increased safety and personal satisfaction are well worth the time and effort of advanced instruction. Schools, colleges, and several national organizations conduct courses in swimming and diving.

Games and sports played in the water offer much fun to participants. Family participation in childhood games adapted to the water adds many hours of happiness to backyard pool or beach activities.

Life Saving

Strong swimmers with good endurance should be encouraged to qualify as certified life savers. Several national organizations have carefully prepared courses in life saving. Families owning backyard pools or participating in boating and general aquatic activities must assume the responsibility for making sure that someone in the family has preparation in life saving and is capable of making a water rescue.

Boating

Boat ownership is within the reach of many today and requires knowledge, skill, and practice to make boating a safe, as well as exciting, aquatic activity. More enjoyment from boating will result if boat owners take time to learn about their craft and the special skills which are necessary. Boatmanship training under the auspices of the U.S. Coast Guard, U.S. Power Squadrons, the Boy Scouts of America, and the American National Red Cross is available for little or no cost.

Competitive Swimming

Individual and relay races, plus diving, are included in dual, triangular and group or championship swimming meets. Races are swum over varying distances, using the backstroke, breaststroke, butterfly, and crawl. Diving is done from 1-meter and 3-meter springboards and from a 10-meter tower. Scoring systems for these meets are published in official rule books (see Bibliography.)

Age-group swimming. Shortly after World War II, the Amateur Athletic Union (AAU) developed an extensive program of competitive swimming for youngsters, termed *Age-Group Swimming.* Avid interest in competitive swimming has developed from this program. It is worthy of consideration by communities interested in providing summer competitive swimming programs for children.

Olympics. Every four years there is an Olympiad which includes swimming and diving competition among nations for both men and women. The program consists of events measured in meters and conducted in pools exactly 50 meters (165 feet) in length. Olympic diving competition consists of springboard diving from the 3-meter stand and platform diving from the 10-meter (33 feet) tower.

Officiating. As interest in competitive swimming continues to grow, there is a need for an increasing number of qualified officials. Those who are interested in competitive swimming or diving can render a valuable community service by assisting as meet officials. It is suggested that contact be made with persons in charge of municipal, private, or agency (i.e., YMCA and American National Red Cross) swimming pools for information on how to qualify as an official.

Skin and SCUBA Diving

The term *skin diving* refers to swimming under water with the use of a face mask for increasing vision and fins for propulsion. A "snorkel," or J-shaped breathing tube, is sometimes used to permit the swimmer to keep his head under water for long periods of time. The length of time the swimmer may remain under water without a snorkel depends upon his breath-holding capacity. When divers use "lungs," mechanical breathing apparatus, they are referred to as

SCUBA (Self-Contained Underwater Breathing Apparatus) *divers.* The apparatus consists of air tanks, which are strapped to the back and connected to a mouthpiece by means of flexible hoses through a special regulator.

Both skin and SCUBA diving contain elements of risk and have caused a considerable number of deaths, even among professional divers. In some states legislation prevents the use of certain kinds of equipment. Unless you are physically fit, do not participate in these activities. A period of specialized preparation before engaging in this activity on your own is a necessity. Use only the best kinds of equipment selected by a qualified expert.

If you are interested in skin and SCUBA diving, enroll in a club or join the "Y" where special classes are conducted. Through inquiry you will be able to locate persons with interest in and expert knowledge of this interesting activity. You are cautioned *not* to venture on your own and become a self-styled expert.

Synchronized Swimming

This popular form of "swimming to music" may be simple backyard enjoyment or the basis for an elaborate school or community water show. The term *synchronized swimming* means performing rhythmical aquatic movements in a planned pattern to selected accompaniment. The techniques selected are geared to the ability of the swimmers; thus everyone may enjoy participating in synchronized swimming.

Swimming strokes and certain aquatic skills, usually called stunts, are the basic types of movement used in synchronized swimming. Standard swimming strokes are adapted or combined to achieve desired effects in rhythm and style. Sculling (see page 27) is the foundation for the performance of most stunts. Synchronized swimming provides a high degree of creativity and challenges you to compose or "write" aquatic "dances." Beginning synchronized swimmers find that if they play a record where it can be heard while swimming they discover strokes and stunts that fit the music.

Information on synchronized swimming is usually available at your local "Y," community center, and college swimming club.

Water Skiing

Not only is water skiing fun, exciting, and thrilling, but it is easy to learn the fundamentals. It is vital that water skiing be learned under the tutelage of a qualified instructor. Life jackets must be worn at all times. Water skiing should be engaged in only by persons who are safe deep-water swimmers.

Surf Swimming

Swimming in the ocean is considerably different from pool or lake swimming. The waves are bigger, the water is salty and generally murky, there are fish, crabs, and other sea animals to be tolerated, and there are currents and eddies that must be reckoned with. With travel simplified today, surf swimming is possible for even "land-locked" Midwesterners.

Because surf swimming can be dangerous, it is important that you swim only at beaches supervised by life guards. Most beaches are roped off to indicate safe areas. Swimming beyond this area is not only prohibited but is foolish. Pay heed to the water temperature and avoid long periods of immersion in water below 70°–75° F. Cold water tends to cause cramps, which often lead to a need for assistance.

Aquatic Safety Rules

The ability to swim provides you with an entree to the exciting world of water sports and boating activities. For personal safety as well as for the safety of others follow these rules:

Encourage at least one adult member of your family to secure life saving training.

Check the opportunities in your local community for participation in aquatic activities.

Find out all you can about a sport before you engage in it. Check your level of swimming ability against that suggested by the experts.

Consult qualified sources for information about each sport (see the Bibliography at the end of the book).

Get started under the tutelage of a qualified instructor when you engage in specialized aquatic activities.

Secure help from an expert when purchasing equipment for skin and SCUBA diving.

A SWIMMER'S RESPONSIBILITY

By now you are aware of the magnitude of aquatic activities. The inherent dangers of participation in and mushrooming growth of water sports create a need for vigorous and wise leadership. Although considerable responsibility rests with professionally prepared leaders as well as with governmental officials, all persons who can swim have a stake in guiding the development of aquatics and protecting participants. Adults are obligated to exercise the needed direction and leadership in aquatics.

FAMILY RESPONSIBILITY

Opportunities should be provided for every member of the family to learn to swim well enough to protect themselves and to be aware of safety measures around water. Children should be educated concerning their conduct in and around water. One adult member of each family should have training in life saving and aquatic emergency measures.

With rapidly growing interest in family camping in state and national parks containing large natural bodies of water, more and more families are enjoying aquatic activities. However, risks are ever present and parents must be mindful of them. Constant vigilance of children's participation in aquatics is required if a happy vacation is not to end in tragedy. Engage only in those aquatic activities for which your family is thoroughly prepared.

The swimming pool industry is rapidly making backyard pool ownership a common phenomenon. As construction techniques become refined, an excellent backyard pool can be purchased for a cost equal to that of a new automobile. Prospective pool owners are cautioned to deal only with reputable pool builders and to provide adequate safeguards in accordance with local ordinances. In addition to carrying an adequate amount of liability insurance, the home pool owner should provide gate-locked fences and an automatic water-entry detection alarm. Important also is a prudent attitude of providing adult supervision inside the pool enclosure whenever the pool is in use. It is necessary that with a backyard pool one adult member of the family be trained in life-saving techniques.

COMMUNITY RESPONSIBILITY

Every community should provide means for learning to swim. Ideally, a learn-to-swim program should be a part of the elementary school physical education curriculum, since children generally do not have an undue fear of water and learn to swim quickly. If such a school program is not possible, then good instructional programs should be provided in community sponsored year-round programs. A third choice is a summertime program.

Most communities today have access to some form of aquatic activity. Community owned and operated facilities should be under the direct supervision of personnel trained in aquatics. Persons with experience in physical education, which includes aquatics, and those certified by the American National Red Cross, usually are qualified to conduct an aquatic program. One tragedy is not worth employing unqualified personnel. Insist upon safety first.

Certain legislation relative to boating and the use of all swimming areas, public or private, is essential for safety. Endorse legislation where it is needed. In addition, professional recreation and aquatic leaders need your support and assistance to carry on research and to provide your community with the legal structure to insure safe and enjoyable aquatic programs.

Only as you participate wholeheartedly and intelligently in assuming your share of responsibility will the wonderful world of water sports be safe and rewarding to all participants.

EVALUATION

7

Evaluating swimming performance and knowledge is a constant process and is not reserved only for the time after the fundamentals are mastered. Therefore to help you in the process of continuous evaluation this chapter includes weekly goals and a series of short-answer study and review questions. These devices can be used to determine which skills you have mastered and which skills you need to practice.

Beginning Swimmer Check List

Together with an instructor check or date the appropriate spaces and make notes in the "remarks" column to direct your future practice (see example below.) Only when checks have been recorded in all blocks in the "safe" column can you consider yourself a swimmer —a beginning swimmer.

| Item | Evaluation | | | |
	No Skill	Doubtful	Safe	Remarks
Safety Rules				
Scientific Foundations				
Step 1: Breath control				
Step 2: Tuck Float Prone Float	9/9	9/12	9/15	Take bigger breath
Step 3: Human stroke				
Step 4: Back Float				
Step 5: Beginning back- stroke				
Step 6: Position changes				
Step 7: Treading Water				
Step 8: Jump Dive				
Step 9: Composite skill test				

Composite Skill Test

Schools and colleges have various composite skill tests or deep water tests. The purpose of all such tests is to qualify persons to swim, WITH COMPETENT SUPERVISION, in deep water, and to signify that they are ready for advanced instruction. Passing such a test does not mean that a person is safe to swim in any kind of water at any time. Passing the following test satisfies only beginning swimmer requirements.

> Jump or dive into deep water. Tread water for one minute. Using any stroke in the prone position, swim 25 yards. Return to the starting position, using any stroke on the back. Float motionlessly for one minute. Then continue swimming until a total of 5 minutes has elapsed from the start of the test.

STUDY AND REVIEW QUESTIONS

1. Name three health or medical conditions which might cause limited swimming activity.

2. Describe essential foot hygiene in relation to the use of a swimming pool.

3. Why should soap showers be required before using a pool?

4. What is a cramp? What procedures should be followed to release a cramp?

5. Under what conditions, other than from the direct rays of the sun, may an individual become sunburned?

6. What negative actions affecting a beginning swimmer's ability result from fear?

7. Explain the difference in "space orientation" in walking and in swimming.

8. Define relaxation as it applies to swimming.

9. Name two reasons why it is important not to become over-fatigued when learning how to swim.

10. State Newton's Third Law of Motion. Give an example of this law as it applies to swimming.

11. Give an example of the use of resultant forces applied to a swimming action.

12. Define recovery phase. Give an example of a recovery phase in a swimming stroke.

13. Define power phase. Give an example of a power phase in a swimming stroke.

14. What is the principle of buoyancy which enables the body to maintain swimming positions?

15. What safety precautions should a non-swimmer utilize in learning to swim?

16. Define "aquatic breathing."

17. List the three important cues to remember in recovering to a standing position from the face float.

18. What is the arm-leg coordination of the human stroke?

19. In what position is the swimmer when a back float is correctly executed?

20. Briefly describe the mechanics of sculling.

21. Briefly describe the process of turning from swimming the human stroke to swimming the beginning backstroke.

22. What should be the action of the ankles and knees when jumping into water four feet deep?

23. What is the minimum depth of water in which it is safe to learn to dive?

24. Describe the correct arm position when learning to dive.

25. Describe the body position for the elementary backstroke with reference to the relationship of the head, trunk, and hips.

26. To what position do the arms reach in the recovery of the elementary backstroke?

27. Describe the coordinated movement of arms and legs when swimming the sidestroke.

28. In the crawl, how many kicks are there to each complete arm cycle?

29. Describe the power action of the arms when swimming the crawl.

30. In the crawl, when is a breath taken in relation to the arm motion on the same side as the breathing?

31. What is the direction of force in the backstroke arm action?

32. What is meant by the term *windmill* when used in connection with the backstroke?

33. What are two important differences and two important similarities of the crawl kick and the backstroke kick?

34. Briefly describe the count you would use in explaining the co-ordination of the backstroke.

35. With what part of the leg is pressure applied in the power action of the breaststroke kick?

36. Briefly describe the coordination of the breaststroke.

37. Briefly describe the arm action of the butterfly stroke.

38. Describe the arm-leg coordination of the butterfly stroke.

39. What is the theory of "drownproofing"? Briefly describe the six steps of executing the drownproofing technique.

40. Name two strokes that may be used when swimming under water.

41. About how much distance should be covered on each thrust from the pool bottom in progressive bobbing?

42. On what law of physics is progressive bobbing based?

43. What two forces carry the body down when executing a head-first surface dive?

44. List five common sense rules to prevent water emergencies.

45. Define and describe an "on-shore" rescue.

46. What should be the proportion of trained life savers in the general population?

47. Prepare three consecutive daily practice schedules designed to improve your swimming proficiency.

48. Define SCUBA. What special precautions are necessary before participating in this activity?

49. Describe the necessary safety precautions that should be observed by the owners of home pools.

50. List three books you would purchase for the family in the area of aquatics. Tell why you would select each book.

Table of Swimming Objectives

The table of objectives on the following two pages is designed to suggest a progression of skills to practice and goals to meet to assure steady progress in becoming a competent swimmer. These objectives suggest possible accomplishments for those receiving instruction three days per week and who practice on the alternate days. Daily practice periods are encouraged. Some persons will progress faster than others and it should be remembered that these objectives are to be used only as a guide for practice, not as a fixed schedule.

SWIMMING OBJECTIVES

(Based upon instruction three times per week and practice twice a week)

Activity	Page Reference	Weekly Goals							
		1	2	3	4	5	6	7	8
Breath holding	15	30 sec	40 sec	50 sec	60 sec				
Rhythmical breathing and bobbing	16-17	10 breaths	20 breaths	30 breaths	40 breaths	unlimited			
Tuck float and recovery	18-19	20 sec	40 sec	50 sec	60 sec				
Face float, glide and recovery	19-20	5 ft	10 ft	15 ft					
Human stroke	21-22	10 yards	15 yards	25 yards	40 yards	50 yards			
Back float and recovery	23-26	20 sec	40 sec	1 min	2 min	unlimited			
Beginning backstroke	26-28	—	10 yards	15 yards	25 yards	40 yards	50 yards		
Turning around	29-30	—	4 times	8 times	unlimited				
Turning over	30-31	—	4 times	8 times	unlimited				
Treading water	31-32	—	15 sec	30 sec	1 min	2 min			

Skill	Pages								
Jumping	33	—	—	—	5 times from pool side	5 times from 1-meter board	*optional* 5 times from 3-meter board	—	—
Diving	34-35	—	—	—	5 times from pool side	*optional* 5 times from 1-meter board	—	—	—
Deep water swimming	14	—	—	—	1 min	3 min	4 min	5 min	—	—
Composite Skill Test	78	—	—	—	—	Try	Try	Pass	—	—
The objectives below are suitable for elementary or intermediate swimming instruction.									
Elementary Backstroke	37-40	—	—	—	—	—	15 yards	25 yards	50 yards	—
Crawl	44-47	—	—	—	—	—	15 yards	25 yards	50 yards	50 yards
Sidestroke	40-43	—	—	—	—	—	—	15 yards	25 yards	—
Drownproofing	59-61	—	—	—	—	—	—	2 min	5 min	10 min
Backstroke	48-51	—	—	—	—	—	—	15 yards	25 yards	50 yards
Breaststroke	51-55	—	—	—	—	—	—	—	15 yards	25 yards
Underwater Swimming	62-64	—	—	—	—	—	—	—	10 feet	20 feet
Surface Dive	66-68	—	—	—	—	—	—	—	5 times	10 times
Progressive Bobbing	64-66	—	—	—	—	—	—	—	—	5 times
Butterfly	55-58	—	—	—	—	—	—	—	—	15 yards

GLOSSARY

Aquatics: Activities related to water; boating, diving, life saving, skin and SCUBA diving, surfing, synchronized swimming, and water skiing are some of these activities.

Beat: A phase of the crawl or backstroke, such as the upward thrust of the leg; generally there are six beats (kicks) in one complete crawl or backstroke cycle.

Buoy: A device used to assist a swimmer in remaining afloat.

Buoyancy: That property of a body that makes floating possible.

Catch: The act of applying pressure to the water with the hand just prior to exerting propulsive force.

Cycle: The complete movement of both arms and both legs in the execution of a stroke.

Dolphin kick: A simultaneous up-and-down, undulating motion of the legs; used in the butterfly stroke.

Entry: The movement of the body or a part of the body into the water.

Extension: The straightening of the body at any joint.

Flexion: The bending of the body at any joint.

Form: A coordinated and prescribed movement of the body or parts of the body.

Freestyle: Used synonymously with crawl, but refers to any type of stroke to be used in certain competitive swimming events.

Glide: Movement through the water without action.

Kickboard: A small wooden or plastic board (about 10″ x 18″) used to support the arms while practicing various leg actions; often referred to as a *flutter board*.

Marina: A man-made harbor for boats consisting of piers, mooring and service (food, fuel, repair) establishments.

Medley: A combination, usually of strokes; also a combination of distances in certain types of relay races.

Meet: Competition between two or more teams or competition between individuals in which a series of competitive events is planned.

Natatorium: An enclosure containing a swimming pool.

Pace: The spacing of energy or effort over a period of time.

Press: The effort of the arms to move the body through the water.

Prone: A horizontal position with the front of the body down.

Pull: See *Press.*

Recovery: The movement of the arms or legs from the end of the power phase of a stroke to the beginning of a new power phase.

Ride: The carrying of a part of the body at the surface of the water.

SCUBA: Self-Contained Underwater Breathing Apparatus.

Sinker: One who does not float motionlessly.

Slip: The act of losing power when exerting force against the water because of improper action.

Start: The diving entry in the water used in swimming races.

Stroke: A pattern of arm and leg action which moves the body through the water.

BIBLIOGRAPHY

American National Red Cross. *Life Saving and Water Safety*, 2nd ed. Philadelphia: P. Blakiston's Sons & Co., 1937.

> An inexpensive but thorough approach to personal safety in the water and all forms of rescue. Excellent on near drowning accidents. Used as a text for the American Red Cross Senior Life Saving course.

————. *Swimming and Diving*. Philadelphia: P. Blakiston's Sons & Co., Inc., 1938.

> A classic in the field. One of the first books which describe swimming from an historical point of view and show the development of a variety of swimming strokes. Thoroughly analyzes the styles of swimming and springboard diving.

Armbruster, David A., Sr., Robert H. Allen, and Bruce Harlan. *Swimming and Diving*, 3rd ed. St. Louis: C. V. Mosby Co., 1958.

> A carefully written book based on research and study by experts. Excellent for advanced students and as a reference for all levels of ability.

Conference for National Cooperation in Aquatics. *The Science of Skin and SCUBA Diving*, Rev. ed. New York: Association Press, 1959.

> The result of a working group at the Fourth Annual Meeting of the CNCA at Yale University. The many authorities who have contributed to this book make it a highly recommended addition to the aquatic library for those who are interested in this field.

Gabrielsen, M., Betty Spears, and B. W. Gabrielsen. *Aquatics Handbook*. Englewood Cliffs, N.J.: Prentice-Hall, Inc., 1960.

> Sixteen experts have contributed to this *Handbook*, which incorporates all major aquatic activities except power boating. A description of the basic techniques in the execution of each activity make it an important addition to the family aquatic library.

Guides and Handbooks

Several organizations publish information about current rules, records, officiating techniques, and recent developments in aquatics.

The following publications are noteworthy:

Official Aquatics Guide. Division of Girls and Women's Sports. American Association for Health, Physical Education and Recreation. 1201–16th St., N.W., Washington, D.C.

Official AAU Swimming Handbook. The Amateur Athletic Union, 233 Broadway, New York, N.Y.

Official NCAA Swimming Guide. The National Collegiate Bureau, Box 757, Grand Central Station, New York, N.Y.

Spears, Betty. *Beginning Synchronized Swimming.* Minneapolis: Burgess Publishing Co., 1958.

Completely illustrated and clearly analyzed basic skills in synchronized swimming. An introduction to composition and planning informal water shows.

U.S. Coast Guard Auxiliary. *Basic Seamanship and Safe Boat Handling.* Coast Guard Auxiliary National Board, 1959.

A manual of eight lessons in seamanship and boat handling. Includes illustrations of techniques and information pertaining to navigation and sail and motor boat operation.